THE
PROBLEM
OF
EVIL

What People Are Saying about

HOW NOW SHALL WE LIVE?

"A bracing challenge—just what the Christian church needs to hear in the new millennium. A very powerful book."—**The Honorable Jack Kemp**

"How Now Shall We Live? is truly inspiring for those who want to restore to our culture the values that made America great. It reminds us that we must not only defend what we believe, but also inspire others to give witness to the truth along-side us."—**The Honorable Tom DeLay**, Majority Whip, United States House of Representatives

"The singular pleasure that comes from it is its absolute—learned—refusal to give any quarter to the dogged materialists who deny any possibility that there was a creator around the corner. This is a substantial book, but the reader never tires, as one might from a catechistic marathon. The arguments are cogently and readably presented."—**William F. Buckley** in *National Review*

"The newest—and certainly the most important—of Charles Colson's books . . . the essence of this book is that the Christian faith is not just a theory, not just a system, not just a framework. It is an all-consuming way of life, robustly applicable to every minute of every day of the rest of your life."—*World*

"There is something wrong with the historical development of the evangelical mind, . . . a lopsidedness, a prodigious development of one divine gift coupled with the atrophy of another. . . . We know a great deal about saving grace, but next to nothing—though it is one of our doctrines—about common grace. The ambition of Charles Colson and Nancy Pearcey is to do something about this lopsidedness, to strike a blow against the scandal of the evangelical mind. . . . A highly intelligent book, it is not ashamed to speak to ordinary folk."
—*First Things*

"How Now Shall We Live? is brilliantly lit by its in-depth and succinct diagnosis of the modern mentality . . . an intelligent and thoroughgoing critique from a Scriptural perspective, of the American/Western culture. . . . The book is a veritable mosaic of precious intellectual gems, artistically designed by Charles Colson and Nancy Pearcey. . . . This book is a virtual 'must' for the thinking Orthodox reader."—*DOXA*, a quarterly review serving the Orthodox Church

"A magnum opus in the best Schaefferian tradition. It is clearly intended to be . . . a handbook for today's Christian. . . . The authors presuppose that Christianity is more than just a religion of personal salvation: it involves a total world-and-life view."—*Christianity Today*

DEVELOPING
A CHRISTIAN
WORLDVIEW OF

THE
PROBLEM
OF
EVIL

CHARLES
COLSON
AND NANCY PEARCEY

Tyndale House Publishers, Inc.
Wheaton, Illinois

Visit Tyndale's exciting Web site at www.tyndale.com

The Problem of Evil

Designed by Kelly Bennema

Edited by Lynn Vanderzalm and MaryLynn Layman

The text for this book is composed of chapters 15–29 of *How Now Shall We Live?* by Charles Colson and Nancy Pearcey. The stories in this book are based on facts resulting from extensive research and from interviews with many of the main characters involved. However, some of the secondary characters in the stories are fictionalized or composite characters; any resemblance to real characters is purely coincidental. In addition, events and circumstances may have been rearranged for dramatic purposes.

Library of Congress Cataloging-in-Publication Data

Colson, Charles W.
    Developing a Christian worldview of the problem of evil / Charles Colson and Nancy Pearcey.
        p. cm. — (Developing a Christian worldview)
    Includes bibliographical references.
    ISBN 0-8423-5584-7 (pbk.)
    1. Redemption. 2. Sin. 3. Good and evil. 4. Progress—Religious aspects—Christianity.
5. Apologetics. I. Pearcey, Nancy. II. Title.
BT775.C65 2001
231'.8—dc21   2001002409

Printed in the United States of America

06   05   04   03   02   01
7   6   5   4   3   2   1

CONTENTS

INTRODUCTION:
WHAT IS A WORLDVIEW?

The way we see the world can change the world.

Our choices are shaped by what we believe is real and true, right and wrong, good and beautiful. Our choices are shaped by our worldview.

The term *worldview* may sound abstract or philosophical, a topic discussed by pipe-smoking, tweed-jacketed professors in academic settings. But actually a person's worldview is intensely practical. It is simply the sum total of our beliefs about the world, the "big picture" that directs our daily decisions and actions. And so understanding worldviews is extremely important to how we live—to know how to evaluate everything from the textbooks in our classrooms to the unspoken philosophy that shapes the message we hear on *Oprah*, from the stories and characters shown in contemporary movies to the lyrics in the music we listen to.

The basis for the Christian worldview, of course, is God's revelation in Scripture. Yet sadly, many believers fail to understand that Scripture is intended to be the basis for all of life. In the past centuries, the secular world asserted a dichotomy between science and religion, between fact and value, between objective knowledge and subjective feeling. As a result, Christians often think in terms of the same false dichotomy, allowing our belief system to be reduced to little more than private feelings and experience, divorced from objective facts.

Evangelicals have been particularly vulnerable to this narrow view because of our emphasis on personal commitment. On one hand, this has been the movement's greatest strength, bringing millions to a relationship with Christ. Somewhere in most of our spiritual journeys is a sawdust trail, as there certainly is in mine. I remember as vividly as if it were yesterday that sultry summer night in 1973, in the midst of the Watergate scandal, when I, a former marine captain—often called the "toughest of the Nixon tough guys," the "White House hatchet man"—broke down in tears and called out to God.[1] Apart from that encounter with Christ and assurances of his forgiveness, I would have suffocated in the stench of my own sin. My soul would never have found rest. But this emphasis on a personal relationship can also be evangelicalism's greatest weakness because it may prevent us from seeing God's plan for us beyond personal salvation. Genuine Christianity is more than a relationship with Jesus as expressed in personal piety, church attendance, Bible study, and works of charity. It is more than discipleship, more than believing a system of doctrines about God. Genuine Christianity is a way of seeing and comprehending *all* reality.

It is a worldview.

Understanding Christianity as a total life system is absolutely essential, for two reasons. First, it enables us to make sense of the world we live in and thus order our lives more rationally. Second, it enables us to understand forces hostile to our faith, equipping us to evangelize and to defend Christian truth as God's instruments for transforming culture.

MORAL ORDER

Because the world was created by an intelligent being rather than by chance, it has an intelligible order. As Abraham Kuyper, the great nineteenth-century theologian who served as prime minister of Holland, wrote, "All created life necessarily bears in itself a law for its existence, instituted by God Himself."[2] The only way to live a rational and healthy life is to ascertain the nature of these divine laws and ordinances and then to use them as the basis for how we should live. We tend to understand this principle very well when it comes to the physical order. We know that certain laws exist in the physical world and that if we defy those laws, we pay a steep price. Ignoring the law of gravity can have very unpleasant consequences if we happen to be walking off the edge of a cliff. To live in defiance of known physical laws is the height of folly.

But it is no different with the moral laws prescribing human behavior. Just as certain physical actions produce predictable reactions, so certain moral behavior produces predictable consequences. Hollywood may portray adultery as glamorous, but it invariably produces anger, jealousy, broken relationships, even violence. Defiance of moral laws may even lead to death, whether it is the speeding drunk who kills a mother on her way to the store or the drug addict who contracts and spreads AIDS. No transgression of moral law is without painful consequences.

If we want to live healthy, well-balanced lives, we had better know the laws and ordinances by which God has structured creation. And because these are the laws of our own inner nature, Kuyper notes, we will experience them not as oppressive external constraints but as "a guide through the desert," guaranteeing our safety.[3]

This understanding of life's laws is what Scripture calls wisdom. "Wisdom in Scripture is, broadly speaking, the knowledge of God's world and the knack of fitting oneself into it," says Cornelius Plantinga Jr., president of Calvin Theological Seminary.[4] A wise person is one who knows the boundaries and limits, the laws and rhythms and seasons of the created order, both in the physical and the social world. "To be wise is to know reality and then accommodate yourself to it."[5] By contrast, those who refuse to accommodate to the laws of life are not only immoral but also foolish, no matter how well educated they may be. They fail to recognize the structure of creation and are constantly at odds with reality: "Folly is a stubborn swimming against the stream of the universe . . . spitting into the wind . . . coloring outside the lines."[6]

Precisely. To deny God is to blind ourselves to reality, and the inevitable consequence is that we will bump up against reality in painful ways, just as a blindfolded driver will crash into other drivers or run off the road. We make the bold claim that serious Christians actually live happier, more fulfilled, more productive lives by almost every measure. (Studies are beginning to bear this out.) This simply makes sense. Someone who accepts the contours and limits of the physical and moral order doesn't engage in folly—whether stepping off a cliff or committing adultery or driving drunk.

THE REAL CULTURE WAR

Our calling is not only to order our own lives by divine principles but also to engage the world. We are to fulfill both the *great commission* and the *cultural commission.* We are commanded both to preach the Good News and to bring all things into submission to God's order, by defending and living out God's truth in the unique historical and cultural conditions of our age.

To engage the world, however, requires that we understand the great ideas that compete for people's minds and hearts. Philosopher Richard Weaver has it right in the title of his well-known book: *Ideas Have Consequences.*[7] It is the great ideas that inform the mind, fire the imagination, move the heart, and shape a culture. History is little more than the recording of the rise and fall of the great ideas—the worldviews—that form our values and move us to act.

A debilitating weakness in modern evangelicalism is that we've been fighting cultural skirmishes on all sides without knowing what the war itself is about. We have not identified the worldviews that lie at the root of cultural conflict—and this ignorance dooms our best efforts.

The culture war is not just about abortion, homosexual rights, or the decline of public education. These are only the skirmishes. The real war is a cosmic struggle between worldviews—between the Christian worldview and the various secular and spiritual worldviews arrayed against it. This is what we must understand if we are going to be effective both in evangelizing our world today and in transforming it to reflect the wisdom of the Creator.

WORLDVIEWS IN CONFLICT

The world is divided not so much by geographic boundaries as by religious and cultural traditions, by people's most deeply held beliefs—by worldviews. So argued the distinguished Harvard scholar Samuel Huntington in a celebrated article a few years ago.[8] And Christians would agree. Because we are religious creatures, our lives are defined by our ultimate beliefs more sharply than by any other factor. The drama of history is played out along the frontiers of great belief systems as they ebb and flow.

But if this is so, what does it tell us about the divisions in the world today? Where is the clash of civilizations most bitter?

Huntington predicted a clash between the worldviews of three major traditional civilizations: the Western world, the Islamic world, and the Confucian East. But one of his former students, political scientist James Kurth, took issue with him, contending that the most significant clash would be within Western civilization itself—between those who adhere to a Judeo-Christian framework and those who favor postmodernism and multiculturalism.[9]

I believe Kurth is right. And the reason this conflict within Western culture is so significant is that Western culture may soon dominate the globe. Information technology is rapidly crossing traditional barriers of geography and national boundaries. The fall of the Iron Curtain has opened a large area of the world to Western ideas. Asian and Islamic societies find they cannot insulate themselves from the influx of Western books, movies, and television programs. In Singapore, I met with a Christian cabinet minister who lamented that because Asians associate the West with Christianity, the flood of smut from the West is making his Christian witness difficult. Across the globe, people are complaining about what one French politician described as a "U.S. cultural invasion."[10]

As a result, people around the world are wrestling with the same questions that we face in the States. In Africa, one of the continent's most respected Christian leaders asked for permission to reprint transcripts of my radio program, *BreakPoint*. Though the program is targeted at an American audience, he found that the subjects are the same as those he is dealing with in Africa. Another African Christian leader told me that Western notions of multiculturalism are being used to justify tribalism, and the local church is baffled over how to counter the divisive force. As people in Pakistan get on-line with people in Pennsylvania, America's culture war is increasingly spilling over into other nations.

The sobering conclusion is that our own effectiveness in defending and contending for truth has repercussions across the entire globe. American Christians had better get serious about understanding biblical faith as a comprehensive worldview and showing how it stands up to the challenges of our age.

The three books in this "Developing a Christian Worldview" study series—based on the book *How Now Shall We Live?*—are designed to help you do just that.

Christians must understand the clash of worldviews that is changing the face of society and the world. And we must stand ready to respond as people grow disillusioned with false beliefs and values, and as they begin to seek real answers. We must know not only what our worldview is and why we believe it but also how to defend it. We must also have some understanding of the opposing worldviews and why people believe them. Only then can we present the gospel in language that can be understood. Only then can we defend truth in a way that is winsome and persuasive.

The dangerous myth of the twentieth century is that people are good and getting better. It's a terrible lie. The most chilling horrors of the twentieth century can be traced to this deception. The biblical worldview says quite the opposite, that we had the choice to be good but chose not to be. And the greatest quest of human beings is to answer the questions, Is there any hope? Is there any chance of redemption? These are the questions at the heart of this book.

HOW TO USE THIS BOOK

Although this book, the second in a three-part "Developing a Christian Worldview" series, stands alone, it builds on the book *Science and Evolution,* which looks at the first and most basic worldview questions: *Where did we come from, and who are we?* As we discuss and defend our faith, we need to be equipped to counter the prevailing notion that our universe and world are here by chance and that we humans just happened to evolve from amoebas.

Science and Evolution lays out evidence that our world and its inhabitants are the result of the designing hand of a personal Creator. But it doesn't stop there. As it argues for a creationist worldview, it lays out reasoned arguments showing the flaws in and implications of the naturalist worldview. As humans, we are created in the image of God, meant to glorify God and enjoy him forever.

That's where this book, *The Problem of Evil,* begins. God created a world and a host of creatures, including humans, and deemed that creation "good." But in Eden mankind "fell," and things have never been the same. This raises the second basic worldview question: *What has gone wrong with the world?* And right behind it the third: *What can we do to fix it?* These are the questions addressed in these pages, which explore the deep questions about sin, evil, and suffering. To help you grasp the truths of the Christian worldview, we again, as in *Science and Evolution,* present the ineffectual ways various worldviews cast the problem and show the inadequacy of the promises they make for salvation.

To help you understand, assimilate, and remember the material in these chapters, we've incorporated questions and activities for a six-session group study. Small-group study is one of the most dynamic ways we as Christians can learn together and support each other, not only in exploring our worldview, but also in articulating our beliefs in ways that make sense to people who hold opposing worldviews. At the moment, you may not feel qualified or confident enough to speak out about your worldview, but we hope that your group experience will equip you to become an effective communicator of the truth.

PRACTICAL TIPS

At the beginning of each chapter, you'll find questions to help you focus on key points as you read. We suggest that you highlight or underline as you read, marking points you want to remember and points you want to discuss and clarify with your group. In the text of some chapters, key phrases are already underlined to facilitate reading and discussion.

Each study session covers the material in two or three chapters. At the end of each session-segment you'll find discussion questions. Each set of questions reviews and reinforces the chapter's content. It also draws you to a brief passage of Scripture relevant to the chapter content and/or complementary worldview issues.

We've left some blank space after each question, allowing you to jot notes, but with no clear expectation that you will write down exhaustive answers before you get to the group gathering. The emphasis in this guide is on discussion and group dynamics.

Note that sessions 2 and 4 call for a leader to provide "props" to facilitate discussion. These object lessons and group activities are not simply entertaining time fillers; they are meant to help solidify the truth in your experience. All of us learn and remember things better when we experience them than when we merely hear or read about them. These activities may well trigger the piece of information or reasoned argument that you may need to recall in a later conversation with a skeptic.

This is true also with the suggested role-play activities at the end of study sessions. We suggest you commit ten minutes of each session to this role-play activity; in most of the activities group members practice presenting to a non-Christian what they've learned in this book. Role plays should not be set up in a manner that traumatizes anyone. The goal is encouragement, not intimidation. See further role-play guidelines and instructions in session 1. Role plays can be set up in groups of two or three, or they can be acted out in front of the whole group.

Each session ends with a closing summary question. We suggest that each person in the group verbalize a one-sentence recap: "The one thing that I want to remember from what I read (or heard or did) in this session is . . ."

HAVING AN IMPACT

We trust that this book will provide your group with a forum for lively discussion, a springboard for action, and a tool for accountability. We encourage you to wrestle with ideas presented in the book. Even if you disagree on some points, we're confident that you will come to a deeper understanding of your worldview. Most of all we hope that you are moved to act, to map out goals and strategies for becoming God's redeeming force in this new millennium.

This book is merely a beginning point for you to explore and pursue the truth of what it means to live out a Christian worldview. Take a serious look at the list of resources in the recommended reading section at the end of the book. Choose several titles to deepen your understanding of specific topics that interest you.

We recommend that you continue your study with the remaining book in this three-part series: *The Christian in Today's Culture* (six sessions).

THE GREAT
MODERN MYTH

Certainly nothing offends us more rudely than this doctrine [of original sin], and yet without this mystery, the most incomprehensible of all, we are incomprehensible to ourselves. BLAISE PASCAL

CHAPTER 1

THE TROUBLE WITH US

As you read this chapter, which is the first in a group of chapters that address the second worldview question—What has gone wrong with the world?—keep the following questions in mind:

- What has been the effect on humanity of Adam and Eve's first sin?
- On what did Enlightenment thinkers blame the disorder and suffering they saw in the world?

The first and most fundamental element of any worldview is the way it answers the questions of origins—where the universe came from and how human life began. The second element is the way it explains the human dilemma. Why is there war and suffering, disease and death? These questions are particularly pressing for the Christian worldview, for if we believe that the universe came from the hand of a wise and good Creator, how do we explain the presence of evil? Or, to paraphrase the title of Rabbi Kushner's best-seller, why do bad things happen to good people?[1] If God is both all-loving and all-powerful, why doesn't he use his power to stop suffering and injustice?

ANSWERING THE MOST DIFFICULT QUESTION

No question poses a more formidable stumbling block to the
Christian faith than this, and no question is more difficult for
Christians to answer.

Yet the biblical worldview does have an answer, and it accounts
for universal human experience better than any other belief system. Scripture teaches that God created the universe and created
us in his image, created us to be holy and to live by his commands.
Yet God loved us so much that he imparted to us the unique dignity of being free moral agents—creatures with the ability to make
choices, to choose either good or evil. To provide an arena in
which to exercise that freedom, God placed one moral restriction
on our first ancestors: He forbade them to eat of the tree of the
knowledge of good and evil. The original humans, Adam and
Eve, exercised their free choice and chose to do what God had
commanded them not to do, and they rejected his way of life and
goodness, opening the world to death and evil. The theological
term for this catastrophe is the Fall.

In short, the Bible places responsibility for sin, which opened
the floodgates to evil, squarely on the human race—starting with
Adam and Eve, but continuing on in our own moral choices. In
that original choice to disobey God, human nature became morally distorted and bent so that from then on humanity has had
a natural inclination to do wrong. This is the foundation of the
doctrine that theologians call *original sin,* and it haunts humanity
to this day. And since humans were granted dominion over
nature, the Fall also had cosmic consequences as nature began to
bring forth "thorns and thistles," becoming a source of toil, hard-
ship, and suffering. In the words of theologian Edward Oakes,
we are "born into a world where rebellion against God has already
taken place and the drift of it sweeps us along."[2]

The problem with this answer is not that people find it unclear
but that they find it unpalatable. It implicates each one of us in

the twisted and broken state of creation. Yet just as sin entered
the world through one man, eventually implicating all humanity,
so redemption has come to all through one man (See Rom.
5:12-21). Righteousness is available to all through belief in
Christ's atoning sacrifice.

The Christian view of sin may seem harsh, even degrading,
to human dignity. That's why in modern times, many influential
thinkers have dismissed the idea of sin as repressive and unen-
lightened. They have proposed instead a *utopian* view that asserts
that humans are intrinsically good and that under the right social
conditions, their good nature will emerge. This utopian view has
roots in the Enlightenment, when Western intellectuals rejected
the biblical teaching of creation and replaced it with the theory
that nature is our creator—that the human race arose out of the
primordial slime and has lifted itself to the apex of evolution.
The biblical doctrine of sin was cast aside as a holdover from
what Enlightenment philosophers disdainfully called the Dark
Ages, from which their own age had so triumphantly emerged.
No longer would people live under the shadow of guilt and moral
judgment; no longer would they be oppressed and hemmed in by
moral rules imposed by an arbitrary and tyrannical deity.

But if the source of disorder and suffering is not sin, then where
do these problems come from? Enlightenment thinkers concluded
that they must be the product of the environment: of ignorance,
poverty, or other undesirable social conditions; and that all it
takes to create an ideal society is to create a better environment:
improve education, enhance economic conditions, and reengineer
social structures. Given the right conditions, human perfectibility
has no limits. And so was born the modern utopian impulse.

Yet which of these worldviews, the biblical one or the modern
utopian one, meets the test of reality? Which fits the world and
human nature as we actually experience it?

One can hardly say that the biblical view of sin is unrealistic, with its frank acknowledgment of the human disposition to make wrong moral choices and inflict harm and suffering on others. Not when we view the long sweep of history. Someone once quipped that the doctrine of original sin is the only philosophy empirically validated by thirty-five centuries of recorded human history.

UTOPIANISM AS IRRATIONAL

By contrast, the "enlightened" worldview has proven to be utterly irrational and unlivable. The denial of our sinful nature, and the utopian myth it breeds, leads not to beneficial social experiments but to tyranny. The confidence that humans are perfectible provides a justification for trying to make them perfect . . . *no matter what it takes.* And with God out of the picture, those in power are not accountable to any higher authority. They can use any means necessary, no matter how brutal or coercive, to remold people to fit their notion of the perfect society.

The triumph of the Enlightenment worldview, with its fundamental change in presuppositions about human nature, was in many ways the defining event of the twentieth century, which explains why the history of this era is so tragically written in blood. As William Buckley trenchantly observes: Utopianism "inevitably . . . brings on the death of liberty."[3]

The reasons for this will emerge in the heartwrenching story that follows. To some people, at least initially, this might seem to be a story of misguided do-gooders or a crazy cult. But bear with us, for it is much more than that. It is a cautionary tale, revealing how easy it is to succumb to the great utopian myth, with all its horrifying consequences.

A BETTER WAY
OF LIVING?

As you read, keep the following questions in mind:

- At various stages of Meg and Jack's journey, what appeal did Synanon have to them?
- What warning signs that something was amiss did Meg and Jack ignore?
- When Meg's "eyes were opened," what did she regret?

A LAWYER'S OFFICE, SAN FRANCISCO, 1977

The day Meg Broadhurst walked into my law office and said, "I want you to help me get my child back," she immediately had my attention.

"Has your husband abducted your child?" I asked.

"No, it's more complicated than that. My son, Jason, is at Synanon."

Having lived for the past twenty years in the Bay Area, I had heard of the organization called Synanon, mostly as a drug-rehabilitation program. Although the group had started out in Los Angeles in the late 1950s, they now had a center in Oakland and another up in Tomales Bay, an hour and a half north of the city.

As a family court lawyer, I had heard a lot of strange stories, but the one Meg told me took the prize. At first, after she admitted her own history of alcohol and drug abuse, I wondered whether she might be delusional. Could this really be happening less than two hours from San Francisco?

As much as Meg tried to conceal it, she had a desperate air about her—and a frightfully dark tale to tell. But let her tell her story. . . .

MEG'S STORY

Okay, I'll be honest with you. I got my family involved in Synanon. But first you need to know a little about me and my husband, Jack.

I met Jack at one of my parents' parties in Malibu. He wasn't like the surfers I had been hanging around with. He worked in real estate, and he had something more on his mind than shooting the curl on the north coast of Oahu. When we started dating, he treated me as if I expected more from him than drinking sangria and groping in sleeping bags. His style appealed to my serious side—the part that took me to UCLA to study English. That's where I was at the time, when I wasn't hanging out at the beach. The idea that I could date a man who had ambitions and who thought of the future—and please my parents at the same time—came to me like an epiphany. I could date Jack Broadhurst. I might even marry Jack Broadhurst.

Jack was always telling me how free I was. Maybe I was too young for my age, but he was definitely too old for his, and as we fell in love, it brought out his little-boy side. I think he married me out of gratitude for that. And I married him because I didn't see how else I would ever get my life organized. The rich kids I grew up with thought life would be one endless summer, but something kept telling me that couldn't be real. Besides, I admired Jack. He put on a suit, coped with the real world, and acted . . . well, like a man.

When we got married, we moved into this amazing place in the Malibu Colony. So there I was, still a senior at UCLA, but living in a house on the beach and driving a Porsche. Our first year was so much fun. I didn't have anything to do but study for my classes and cook dinner for my husband. When he came home, we ate, smoked dope, drank wine, and enjoyed each other.

But after I graduated, Jack wanted to go out more, especially to Hollywood parties where he could meet future clients for his high-end real estate business. I hated those parties, and the only way I got through them was to do a few lines of cocaine in the bathroom and then keep drinking tequila. I played the spacey surfer chick while Jack was off in the corner trying to score a one-nighter. By then, you see, Jack and I had settled on an "open marriage"—he could sleep around, and I could "use."

The problem was that when I drank, I didn't stop. And with enough money and enough Bloody Mary and Margarita mix, I really didn't have to—except to get a buzz from the Peruvian powder. Not until the night Jack found me crashed on the floor of someone's bathroom.

That's when we moved to San Francisco and Jack started selling commercial properties downtown. I *really* didn't know what to do with myself on Nob Hill, but I knew I couldn't drink or use, so I spent my time in Alcoholics Anonymous meetings and tried to do the organic health thing. I wanted to be an earth mother, or at least a regular mother, and that's when we had our son, Jason, my little boy that I want you to get back for me. My baby was so wonderful and such a handful, and I went back and forth between loving him to death and wanting to escape all the diapers and drudgery.

Then I heard about these Game Clubs—a kind of AA meeting run by a group called Synanon. People in AA didn't exactly know what to do with someone like me who was attracted to both alcohol and drugs, but Synanon did.[1]

Synanon's Game Club was like an AA meeting except that you could say anything you wanted. You didn't have to talk just about yourself. You could attack people for lying about their addiction or rationalizing their behavior—giving them a "haircut," it was called. No comments were off-limits in the Game.

Once I started talking at the Game Club, I just could not shut up, and those sessions were wild. I loved inviting Jack there and hearing people just blister him for his uptight, businessman ways. And it was amazing, you know, because he actually liked it, too. Somehow when he was inside the Game, he was able to tell me things about our relationship that he never could say otherwise. He needed to know that I really loved him, for one thing. And by that time, I did.

I guess having a kid was changing both of us, and I wanted us to be a real family—to love each other and be good parents to our child. I remember the night I told Jack in the Game, "No more open marriage. No more sleeping around. I don't want that anymore." The other Synanon Game Club members really affirmed what I was saying. They could see how much I wanted our marriage to work.

When we went home that night, Jack called me into Jason's room. As we looked at our five-year-old son sleeping so peacefully, all curled up and snug, Jack whispered to me, "I take thee, Meg, to be my lawfully wedded wife, to have and to hold. . . ." He gave the whole speech, all the vows, the traditional ones that we hadn't even used at our wedding.

After that, Jack and I became so tight. It was as if we fell in love all over again, only this time better, much better. And it was because of Synanon.

Then we heard that Synanon had formed live-in communities, and people like us from the Game Club were beginning to move into them, especially the Tomales Bay facility. The idea really appealed to me, but I never thought Jack would do it. He was Mr.

Money. His idea of a high was taking a building with a bad leasing percentage and selling it within a year for twice what he paid. He could do it, too. Jack knows when a property is basically sound and just needs window-dressing upgrades, and he knows when a bad, old building is just a bad, old building. I have to admit he's a genius at what he does.

But Jack was starting to talk about wanting something more out of life, too, and one day he said to me, "You want to move to Synanon? I mean, like permanently?"

I couldn't believe he was serious. But he was.

The head of the San Francisco Game Club had told him that Synanon was interested in recruiting Gamers for executive positions. They needed someone like Jack to help them develop their properties. He would have to do the pots and pans for about a week, like all new members of the community, but then they would move him back into the work he loved.

"Meg," he told me, "why don't we move to a community where we can concentrate on us and on Jason? If there's really a better way of living, maybe we ought to try it."

I never thought I would hear those words come out of Jack's mouth. First the renewed wedding vows and now this! I agreed, and within three months, we moved to Tomales Bay. That was in March of 1973, and that's when this whole story really gets started.

The first time I saw Tomales Bay, I thought, *I'm going to be living in a Japanese landscape painting! It's beautiful.*

Synanon's property there overlooks the water, and up until a couple of years ago, Tomales was the organization's corporate headquarters. That's moved to Badger now, but the warehouse at the center of Synanon's main business, Advertising Gifts and Premiums (ADGAP), is still at Tomales. The place is like a little self-enclosed city. There are about five hundred people still living there, and it has medical clinics, a barbershop, sewage treatment plants, a movie theater, artists' studios—everything.

When Jack and I first arrived, I thought Charles Dederich, the founder of Synanon, was some kind of guru. He invited Jack and me to have a private conference with him, and we were so excited to meet with the old man himself. We had seen him before, of course, in the Game Temple, the special building devoted to the AA-like sessions at Tomales. But we had never met him in person.

That first meeting, he totally blew us away. He put his arm around Jack and said, "Now I know what you're asking yourselves. Have we made the right choice, moving in here with all these drunks and head-cases? Meg had a problem, I understand, but obviously she's now highly functional. So you're asking, Is this the right thing for our family?

"I'll tell you why you came here, Jack. You know what's inside you. You know that there's a desire to live as you've never lived before, and somehow you just can't get to do it in the world outside Synanon. You know you're alive inside the Game Club in a way you never are outside it.

"Let me tell you why that is. It's because the thing inside you, your real self, is total energy. It drives toward life in its highest sense. It's restless, and it stays restless until it finds fulfillment."

Then Dederich quoted his favorite lines from Ralph Waldo Emerson, the same ones we would always quote at the outset of every Game: " 'As long as a man willingly accepts himself, he will continue to grow and develop his potentialities. As long as he does not accept himself, much of his energies will be used to defend rather than to explore and actualize himself.'

"Here at Synanon you're going to have a chance to accept yourself and use your energies to grow, to be positive, to become a self-actualized person," Dederich said. "Why can't you do that on the outside? Because our whole society fosters various forms of character disorders. When Synanon first got started back in Ocean Park in 1958, I thought the problem was addiction. But the real problem is character disorder, and it's something everyone suffers from—you, Jack, as much as Meg, even though she was the one with the addiction. You're addicted to other things. Like money and other women—right? There's no shame in it. We're all messed up because of the society we've been raised in.

"But here at Synanon you can tap your inner resources toward absolute fulfillment because you can see through your own disguises in the Game. We can help you be free from all those hangups, all those crusty old ideas of right and wrong that shackle your inner self. We're going to set you free from those outdated rules and conventions that hem you in, so you can finally be your true self. You're going to be free from all your character disorders, and together we can make a healthy community and show the whole world a better way of living."

I remember after that meeting, Jack said, "That man's a genius. No one's ever seen through me like that."

For a while our life at Synanon was everything we dreamed of. We worked ten-day shifts, which is called "being in Motion," and then we had ten days for "Growth," which meant we could go horseback riding, take a swim in Synanon's reservoir, sail on the bay, watch movies, use the libraries, do crafts. We didn't have much money, but we didn't need it.

When people joined, they often gave all their money to Synanon. That's how much they believed in what Synanon was doing. We all got a regular allowance from the organization—pocket money that we called WAM (Walking Around Money). And since we had free use of all Synanon's facilities, we lived as if we were rich.

There wasn't any crime there, either. We could leave our possessions right out in the open and not lock any doors. The whole place was run with only two rules: no violence and no drugs, and that included alcohol and cigarettes. So we had all these people, most of them former addicts and lots of them former criminals, and yet the place was completely peaceful. Dederich kept talking about starting new "Synanon cities" all around the country so we could spread this peaceful new way of life to everyone. We were excited about being involved in such a noble mission.

Jack and I worried at first when people in the Game suggested that we put Jason in the community's boarding school. He was only seven. But we found out that it was common for parents to hand over their kids to the community schools when the children were as young as six months old. The leaders told us it was much healthier for a child to be loved by the whole community, where everyone functions as the child's extended family. That sounded good, and anyway, we saw Jason every night. At least we did at first, until they started night nurseries. We also turned over all of Jason's clothes to the school because the kids there didn't own their clothes; they just took them out of communal bins.

But with other people taking care of Jason, Jack and I did get to spend more time together. That's what really hooked me—the chance for Jack and me to be happy together.

I really became a Synanon fanatic the night Dederich started "Gaming" Jack about his latest fling. You see, I thought Jack had stopped that kind of thing when he recited the wedding vows that night. But he hadn't. We were all in the Game Temple— Dederich in his big chair at the front, wearing his overalls and plaid shirt, and his wife, Betty, next to him in one of her long, flowing gowns.

"I want to introduce Jack Broadhurst," Dederich said to the guests, who came to watch. "Jack's a square. He comes to us from a successful real estate business. He sold it when he decided to join Synanon and invested $100,000 in our corporation. Brought his wife, Meg, and his son, Jason, here, too. I just appointed Jack the director of our Land Development Division." Then Dederich asked, "You like your new job, Jack?"

"What I like," Jack said, "is being part of Synanon Corporation.

I think it's the best investment anyone can make, not only with their money but their lives as well."

Dederich heaved his weight around, away from Jack. "The man really knows how to blow smoke, doesn't he?" Then Dederich asked me, "Meg, do you know exactly why Jack is so pleased with being a big director?"

I knew right away where Dederich was headed. So did everyone else.

"Have you met Trina?" he asked.

"She's Jack's new secretary," I said, playing innocent.

"Trina," Dederich said, "stand up for us."

I had to admit she was pretty. Trina had these striking Italian features, oval eyes, full lips. She was wearing a halter top and miniskirt, and stood as if she was posing for *Vogue* or something, with one knee bent in.

"Tell me, Trina," said Dederich, "before you came to Synanon, what did you do?"

"I was on the road," she said.

"As a rock groupie, right?"

"I provided personal services," she said after a pause.

"Personal services?" said Dederich. "We can call it that if you like, sweetheart. But what it means is, you made yourself available for whatever 'personal services' the band members wanted, and in return, they supplied you with LSD, meth, and quaaludes. Right?"

She crumpled and sat down. "Look, I'm not proud of the way I lived," she muttered.

"None of us are," Dederich said. "But what I want to know is this: Why does my new land development director think *you're* qualified to be his secretary?"

"Hey, Chuck, there were only so many in the applicant pool," Jack said, jumping in.

Dederich bolted around to face Jack. "Hey, Mr. Director," he said mockingly. "I saw to it—I saw to it *personally*—that you had

a legal secretary with twelve years of experience in your candidate
pool. And yet you hired Trina instead. Now just why did you do
that?"

Everyone in the Game Temple started to hoot and holler.
You can't believe the obscene things people scream out in there.

"Okay, okay," bellowed Dederich to calm everyone down.
"The point is, Jack's not going to bring his middle-class, hit-on-
the-secretary act here. He was given a responsible position, and
the first thing he's done has been totally irresponsible. I think
maybe it's back to washing kitchen pots for Jack."

That stopped Jack's cheating on me. He finally became Mr.
Faithful. At least as long as Dederich wanted him to be. But that
part of the story comes later.

Another good thing that happened in Synanon was that I
became a teacher. They let me teach in the boarding school at
Tomales, and I even became head of humanities for the junior
high and high school students. Finally people were taking me
seriously. And I liked teaching because it allowed me to be closer
to Jason since all the schools were in one combined operation.

I remember back in high school, one of my boyfriends said to
me, "You are such a scrumptious muffin." That was me all right,
"the scrumptious muffin" girlfriend, the trippy wife—I played all
these side-dish roles. Nobody knew that I had graduated from
UCLA with honors. But in Synanon, I finally stopped feeling as
if I had to hide my brains. I guess it's because I was pretty straight
compared to everybody else there. For one thing, I hadn't been a
prostitute, like almost half of the women there had been, including Dederich's wife, Betty.

The Synanon schools had been modeled after a sixties-style free
school, like Summerhill, but by the time I started teaching, they
had become rather traditional prep-school institutions. Except
for one thing: We taught the kids to do their own version of the
Game. They would tear into each other for things like not doing

their homework or slacking off on their chores. I thought that was good because it meant the kids kept each other in line. The only thing that bothered me about the school was that Dederich's picture hung on the walls everywhere. It was spooky, like Lenin's picture hanging everywhere in the Iron Curtain countries. And after a while, there was even an expectation that we would teach the kids that they owed their whole lives to Synanon—that their first allegiance wasn't to their parents but to the organization.

In fact, many things began to change after Jack and I had been there about two years. A lot of it was because of the lawsuit.

You see, by that time Dederich had lost interest in helping druggies; he was much more interested in selling Synanon to the world as a new kind of ideal society. He had become an evangelist for the Synanon way of life. The problem is, we were still making a lot of our money by selling corporate giveaway items that presented us as a drug-rehabilitation center. So the *San Francisco Examiner* did an exposé calling Synanon a "racket." Synanon's lawyers turned around and sued the newspaper's parent company, the Hearst Corporation, for using underhanded tactics in gathering their evidence, and we won. Hearst had to pay big bucks.[2]

But the negative publicity hurt the organization, and Dederich decided he would have to redefine its mission. His chief counsel, Dan Garrett, came up with what they thought was a great idea: They would declare Synanon a legal religion. They saw all kinds of advantages: It was better for taxes, and they didn't have to keep trying to bolster the "success rate" with addicts. The success rate really wasn't too good anyway. Most addicts didn't do well if they left Synanon, so most of them were staying on. But if Synanon were a religion, that no longer mattered. As Garrett used to say, "Nobody graduates from a religion." Besides, being a religion meant everyone would have to be a lot more committed and "obey the tenets of the faith"—Garrett actually wrote that in a memo.

In the Game, we spent hours discussing the idea of becoming

a religion, and I had a hard time believing what some people said. They said Chuck was a "god" to them, and Betty was a natural "high priestess." For years, recruits had been welcomed with the slogan "Abandon all and follow Chuck," but I had taken that as a joke. Now I realized that a lot of the old-timers really looked up to Dederich as a Christ figure. We even had a Game where everyone decided Chuck could be called "Savior."[3]

Honestly, I didn't know quite what to think. I guess Synanon *was* like a religion for me in a lot of ways. For instance, in the Game, people frequently rehearsed their life histories—it was called "telling your rotten story"—talking about how hopeless and useless life had been before they joined Synanon. The histories were just like some religious testimonials. But things were going overboard, in my mind. Dederich wrote a book to define the group's beliefs; it was called *The Tao Trip Sermon.* He even wrote a prayer that we were supposed to recite—the Synanon Prayer. Betty got into the act, too, telling people that we were like a seminary, like priests in training, and that we had to accept the Synanon dogma "without any mental reservations"—that we were to "just say 'amen' " to any directive Chuck passed down.

Those were her exact words. She was even starting to *talk* like a high priestess. And anyone who wasn't willing to accept Synanon as a religion was promptly excommunicated.

The Game was really changing, too. Instead of being open and real about what we thought, we started getting pressure to "Game affirmatively." That meant once Chuck or Betty or their insiders had insinuated the Synanon line on anything, everyone was supposed to line up and agree with them. And if we criticized some policy, everyone would jump on us and talk about how grateful we should be for everything Chuck had done for us.

In fact, the group would start dragging up people's pasts, telling them what a mess their lives were before they came to Synanon and how Dederich had saved them. "And *this* is how you repay him?" the group would ask. The pressure was so bad that often the people being attacked would actually start agreeing with the accusations; they would even bring up new faults to confess to the group and start accusing themselves. Creepy. Just like what the communists used to do to break people, getting them to accuse themselves.

By this time, too, Dederich had hooked up an in-house radio network called "the Wire," that was broadcast into every building, every workroom, even the bathrooms, so that every member of Synanon could hear Dederich's thoughts on any subject, any time of the day. You hardly had a moment to think for yourself. Everyone was constantly listening for Chuck's opinion on anything that happened so they could be on the "right" side.

But that wasn't the worst of it. Next came the loyalty tests. Like shaving our heads. Synanon had various forms of punishment that were meted out when we broke the rules, and one of the punishments was having our head shaved. Then, suddenly, it was made clear that *everyone* had to get shaved—permanently—as a kind of proof of their commitment. This was in 1975, and I was still so much a part of things, I got buzzed without much protest. But some of my friends were really upset about losing their hair. Betty tried to make them feel better by telling them, "You cannot be ugly. You are Synanon. You wear the badge of the Religion."[4]

But Synanon was still getting a lot of bad publicity. The article in the *San Francisco Examiner* had tipped off other reporters, and donations began drying up. So Dederich decided he would simply reduce the population, pare it down to those who were absolutely loyal to him. He launched another loyalty test, what he called a "little emotional surgery." He started talking about how couples with children placed a great burden on the community. He told us that raising each child cost Synanon up to $200,000 and how, if we saved that money, we could help juvenile delinquents. "The world is already overpopulated," he would say. "Why should

Synanon members go on breeding when they could selflessly help save children who were already in this miserable world?"[5]

So Chuck ordered all the pregnant women to have abortions. That's when I really started to pull back and wonder about Synanon. There were about five pregnant women there at the time, and one was my best friend, Jean, one of the other teachers. She had wanted a child for the longest time, and she had finally gotten pregnant when she was almost forty years old. She was about five months along when Chuck made his pronouncement, and she really didn't want an abortion. She held out for a while, but everyone kept Gaming her about her loyalty to Synanon, and she couldn't take the pressure.[6]

I tried to talk her out of it, but I remember the day I walked into the school building and knew she had done it. She had been out for a day, and when she came back, she wouldn't look at me, so I knew. She had gone to a Synanon doctor. Now she'll never have any children. And for what? Why?

Dederich knew how upset everyone was over the abortions, but he didn't back off. He let it be known that it would make him very happy if all the men got vasectomies. That meant anyone who wanted to stay in his good graces had better go along— because staying in Chuck's good graces meant better housing, better job assignments, and other perks. If you resisted, you could be demoted and forced to collect garbage or pull weeds.

This was the beginning of the end for Jack and me. I begged Jack, "Please don't do this. Don't get a vasectomy." I wanted to have another baby.

But he knew that his position as land development director was at stake. So he said, "Look, honey, we already have Jason. And besides, I'm getting too old."

"Old? Jack, you're all of thirty-six! Listen, Jack, please," I said. "We've made a mistake. This is completely crazy. We need to leave this place right now."

And the minute I said that—the minute I suggested leaving Synanon—I could see him turn against me. His face got really hard, and he wouldn't listen to me or talk to me. He just shut me out of his life. It was so awful. We had come to Synanon to make our relationship better, but now Synanon was coming between us. Jack is totally dependent on that organization; it's his whole life. He's going to fight me tooth and nail about getting Jason back. As far as he's concerned, Jason doesn't belong to him *or* me; he belongs to Synanon.

So, anyway, he got the vasectomy—I knew he would—and so did every other man in Synanon. Except Dederich himself, of course. Isn't that rich? I know he's laughing at the way he can coerce everyone else to do something he would never lower himself to do. Some couples left Synanon over it, but most of them stayed on, and they were even more committed because of the sacrifice they had made.[7]

But as bad as that is, it's not the worst of it.

After the suit against the Hearst Corporation, Dederich started having fantasies of revenge. Synanon facilities had had break-ins from time to time, especially in Oakland, where a street gang actually came in and started beating up our people for no reason. So Dederich told all the facilities to form security details. They were like volunteer fire departments at first, but in just a short time they got to be like internal police forces. Then Dederich started a group of guards, but really they're more like a small army. They're called the Imperial Marines, and they're made up mostly of juvenile delinquents that government social service agencies send us to rehabilitate.[8] These kids are mean, and they're well armed, too.

On top of this, Dederich started giving tirades over the Wire— the in-house radio network—saying how Synanon was not going to be messed with anymore. He would go on and on about the urban riots of the late 1960s and the crime wave of the 1970s. He

would say that we have to counter violence with violence. Synanon
would "break some legs and kneecaps," if it had to. That's what he
actually said, this former guru of nonviolence.

He even made this part of the Synanon religion. He liked to say
Synanon was becoming an "aggressive, militant" religion and that
we weren't going to mess with turning the other cheek. Instead,
the rule of our religion was "Don't mess with us—it can get you
killed."

And to be fair, I have to warn you that if you take my case,
I'm not sure what might happen, because Dederich gets rabid
when lawyers help former Synanon members get their kids back.
I've heard him say, "I am quite willing to break some lawyer's legs
and next break his wife's legs and threaten to cut their child's arm
off."[9] And he means it, too.

A lot of couples were like me and Jack—one partner wanting
to leave and the other one wanting to stay. I think that's why
Dederich came up with his idea for the biggest loyalty test of all.
He decided marriage was getting in the way of total loyalty to
him, so he decided to get rid of it. Just abolish marriage. To do
this, he decided to split up all the married couples and force them
to hook up with someone else—what he called a "love match."
These would last about three years, and then everyone had to
take a new love match. Dederich himself selected who went with
whom most of the time.[10]

Dederich would hold these big separation ceremonies, where
all the married couples were supposed to thank each other for the
time they had had together and then pair off with someone new.
He started off with his own grown children, to set an example.
His daughter—her name was Jady—really loved her husband, but
she left him to pair up with another man. His son had a harder
time, and Dederich had to threaten to demote him. He said,
"You're not going to get in the way of this movement." As if
Synanon were still some idealistic movement to change the world!

It may have started out that way, but by now it was nothing but personal tyranny. Dederich was stripping all of us of everything we loved, everything we cared about, trying to make us loyal only to him.

He told Jack and me to split, and he put Jack with Trina. Can you believe it? I think he did it to make the point that he could do anything he wanted, even reversing something he had done in the past. For me, Chuck picked Michael Tenney.

I owe Mike a lot, actually. I think he loves his wife, Diane, even more than I love Jack. A lot of people looked up to them as the ideal Synanon couple. Mike's a doctor, Diane's a nurse, and they took care of just about everybody at one time or another at Tomales. I think even Dederich regretted breaking up Mike and Diane, but he couldn't allow exceptions. Diane was so upset, she just walked out of Synanon and never came back. Dederich got on the Wire and ranted about how she was a "splittee"—that's what they call people who leave—and how she had no gratitude, no loyalty, how she was rotten, and on and on. He always did that when anyone left.

Anyway, the first night after I was matched with Mike, I went through the motions; I put on my nightie and waited for Mike to finish taking a shower. I kept thinking of that line from Huxley's *Brave New World:* "Let's do it for the state!" It was like Orwell's *1984,* too, because, I mean, what was the difference between Charles Dederich and Big Brother? Dederich was going for complete control.

Mike came back from the communal showers in his T-shirt and sport shorts, and he shut the door. I've never seen a man look sadder in my entire life, especially walking into a room with a woman waiting for him in bed, and I started laughing.

"What?" Mike asked.

"You. You look like you're about to be drawn and quartered."

He sat down on the side of the bed, and we began to talk. "I've decided to leave Synanon," he said. "I know this may go badly for you. Maybe they'll accuse you of driving me off or something. But I love Diane more than anything in this world, and I want to find her. I hope she'll get back together with me once I'm out."

"Do you know where she is?"

"I haven't talked to her, but she's probably over in Walnut Creek with her sister."

"Look," I said, "you don't have to do this, I know, but if you could just sleep in this room—over there on the couch—for two or three nights, then people would think our 'love match' is working. Then we'll both go at the same time. We'll just split."

Both of us knew how traumatic—even dangerous—it could be to leave Synanon. The Imperial Marines gave one splittee a serious beating. They have a huge cache of weapons, and anyone who leaves gets all kinds of threats. Dederich gets on the Wire and starts condemning splittees and gives out hints that he wouldn't mind if they were hurt. I know it sounds incredible, but the place has turned into an armed camp, a small totalitarian state. I had even heard a rumor about a prison camp they're running in the desert.[11]

Mike and I made our break at the same time, as we planned. Mike and Diane had liquidated all their assets and poured the money into Synanon, so they left with nothing but the clothes on their backs. They lost everything.

As for me, the past month I've been down in Malibu, back with my parents, getting myself together. I've called Jason, and they did let me talk to him. He's twelve now, very independent and, I'm afraid, very foul-mouthed. He thinks he's about to become a cowboy in the Imperial Marines or something, and says he doesn't want to see me anymore. You should hear him. "Mom," he told me, "you don't own me. I belong to Synanon, and that's where you should be, too. You should get your blankety-blank back here." It's as if he's joined the Nazi youth!

He's still a kid, though. He needs his mother. And I need him. I can't believe I gave up so much to be a loyal member of that organization! I've lost years of my life, and I've lost my husband and my child. I realize that Jack's gone, but there's still a chance for Jason. You have to help me get him back. You have to.

"A BETTER WAY OF LIVING"

What you've just read is a dramatized account, and Meg Broadhurst is a fictionalized character. But Synanon, its leader Charles Dederich, and the major figures associated with Synanon are real. The events described here all took place, and the experience of Meg and her family accurately represents the typical fate of those who became involved in Synanon, a countercultural organization devoted to what Dederich liked to call "a better way of living."

Two years after Meg would have been providing this account, a real-life custody battle, similar to the one described in this dramatization, provoked such violence from Charles Dederich that his criminal actions brought Synanon to an end. An attorney named Paul Morantz won a $300,000 judgment against Synanon for its interference in a child-custody case. Afterward, Morantz received so many anonymous threats that he began checking everywhere for traps. One day when he reached into his mailbox, his hand felt as if a nail gun had gone off straight into his palm. He whipped his hand away. Seconds later, a four-and-a-half-foot rattlesnake, its rattles clipped so that it would give no warning, slithered out of the box. Neighbors rushed him to the hospital. Eleven vials of antivenin serum saved his life, but the assault left him with permanent nerve damage.[12]

Through a neighbor's testimony, the attack on Morantz was traced back to Synanon. The two men who set the trap were eventually arrested, along with Dederich himself. All three were indicted, though Dederich was given only a fine and probation.

But the convictions effectively ended Synanon's reign of terror. The community continued to struggle on through the early 1980s, but lawsuits against Synanon for its violent treatment of community members and outsiders, along with the complete collapse of its donation network, demanded that assets be sold off until nothing was left. One by one, former members left Synanon.

Sadly, for many families it was too late. Hundreds of children lost their childhood to Synanon's communal nurseries. Hundreds of parents lost their families, their children's love and affection, and years of their lives to Charles Dederich's "better way of living." It was a utopian dream for an ideal society, and it went the way of all utopian dreams . . . as we shall see.

If the experience of human history from Rousseau to Stalin means anything, it must be that we are stuck, like it or not, with a doctrine—nay the reality—of original sin. EDWARD T. OAKES

CHAPTER 3

SYNANON AND SIN

As you read, keep the following questions in mind:
- By what strategies did Dederich gain cultic control and allegiance?
- What fatal flaw is at the heart of Rousseau's philosophy?
- To Rousseau, what did freedom mean?
- What are the implications of Rousseau's ideas?

Synanon is not just a tale of 1960s idealism gone awry in a small corner of northern California. It is a parable of what happens when men and women reject the biblical teaching of sin and evil and then embrace the great modern myth of utopianism: that human nature is intrinsically good and can form the basis of a perfect society. As political philosopher Glenn Tinder writes, if one acknowledges "no great, unconquerable evils in human nature," then it seems possible to create a heaven right here on earth.[1]

This was exactly the philosophy behind Synanon. And in the events of that small, coercive community, we can see in microcosm just how dangerous that philosophy is. For when we close our eyes to the human capacity for evil, we fail to build the moral boundaries needed to protect us from that evil.

Charles Dederich's desire to free addicts from their destructive behavior began with apparently good intentions. His approach

was inspired, in large part, by the individualism of Ralph Waldo
Emerson, who trusted that the isolated self could find within itself
all the goodness and truth needed for a moral community. This is
what Emerson meant by his celebrated notion of "self-reliance"—
that the self, in its search for truth, must be freed from all external
authority, whether divine revelation, the church, history, or tradition. Emerson announced the dawn of a new age of "every one for
himself; driven to find all his resources, hopes, rewards, society,
and deity within himself."[2]

This utopian vision of a new age shaped Dederich's strategy.
To create isolated, Emersonian individuals among his flock, he
mercilessly attacked all their preconceptions, belief systems, and
moral loyalties. He broke down their emotional reserve in the
vicious free-for-all exchanges of the Game; he severed loyalty to
family and friends by recasting outsiders as "enemies"; he
invaded the private boundaries of the mind with the Wire; and
finally, he destroyed the family, with his enforced policies of
communal nurseries, abortion and vasectomy, and temporary
"love matches."

The idea was that old emotional ties, old loyalties, old thought
patterns must be torn down to make way for new, positive,
healthy patterns to emerge. But what really emerged was total
dependence on a cultic authority figure. When moral convictions
and personal commitments are destroyed, the result is not a great
release of human goodness. Instead, the individual becomes
malleable, controllable by anything or anyone who steps in to
take the place of family, church, and village—and who can then
impose his will and convictions on the isolated individual.

All utopians, no matter how well intentioned, adopt this strategy in one form or another. They start with the promise to liberate the individual from such things as economic oppression or
crime-ridden streets or ancient superstitions. And the bargain is
always the same: Give me power, and I'll use it to create an ideal

society. But, as we saw in the Synanon story, the exchange only brings out the worst in those who have the power, while enslaving those they promised to liberate.

Does the modern utopian worldview, then, produce a rational, sustainable life system? Most emphatically not. It tells us we are good, but it unleashes the worst evil. It promises enlightenment, but it thrusts us into darkness.

The cautionary lesson we must derive from Synanon is that the same pattern can take hold anywhere the utopian myth is accepted. Contrary to comfortable contemporary assumptions, the threat of tyranny did not die in the rubble of the Berlin Wall. The utopian myth lives on. Admittedly there's an enormous difference between a totalitarian state and America's democratic republic, yet the same assumptions that led to the most destructive tyrannies of the twentieth century are at work in our own society. The only difference is the speed at which these ideas are being played out toward their inevitable consequences. While the totalitarian nations have completed the cycle, demonstrating the consequences of utopianism in all their horror, most Western nations are still somewhere in the earlier stages, still couching the utopian vision in humanitarian language.

For example, the denial of sin and responsibility is couched in therapeutic terms, such as the need to "understand" even the worst crimes as a result of a dysfunctional childhood or other circumstances. Symptoms of family breakdown—such as divorce, adultery, and abortion—are defended as expressions of the individual's freedom of choice. Social engineering schemes are dressed up as public compassion. But these are all window dressings, for beneath these explanations lies the same false utopian view we saw played out vividly in the story of Synanon. It is the same worldview that gave rise to modern totalitarianism. As Glenn Tinder writes, "Much of the tragic folly of our times, not only on the part of extremists such as Lenin but also on the part of middle-of-the-road liberals and conservatives, would never have arisen had we not, in our technological and ideological pride, forgotten original sin."[3]

Will the Western nations see through their delusions and change course before it is too late? That is a pressing question raised in the following chapters, where we will probe the consequences of the false worldview of human goodness, in both the totalitarian systems of the East and the welfare state of the West. We will trace this worldview's effects in politics, psychology, crime, welfare, and education, in order to reveal its fatal weaknesses. Against the utopian worldview, we will pose the Christian worldview, which we submit is demonstrably the only philosophy that fits universal human experience.

But first we must look at how the myth of utopianism was born and why it has such a grip on the modern mind. We cannot begin to counter the myth until we understand how the utopian vision came to replace what had been for sixteen centuries the settled understanding of human nature and society. In other words, whatever became of the biblical notion of sin?

ROUSSEAU'S NOTORIOUS NOTION

Whatever became of sin? In 1973, when psychiatrist Karl Menninger posed this provocative question in his best-selling book of that title, he sounded like an Old Testament prophet thundering against the moral relativism of our age.[4] Let's not talk about what's progressive or unprogressive, what's appropriate or inappropriate, he said, cutting through the fog of fashionable cover-up words like a brisk breeze. Let's talk about good and evil, right and wrong.

What did become of sin? Good question. To solve the mystery, we must travel back to the mid–eighteenth century and to the influential writings of a young Swiss-born philosopher named

Jean-Jacques Rousseau. Persuasive ideas are typically launched in the writings of one person who captures and gives expression to what becomes a powerful trend. Such was the case when Rousseau burst upon the European intellectual scene, winning instant notoriety with an essay arguing a surprising thesis: that the progress of civilization had not been beneficial for human beings, but harmful. In its natural state, human nature is good, he contended; people become evil only when they are corrupted by society.

From the time of Aristotle, most philosophers had taught that humans are naturally social and that they fulfill their true nature by participating in the civilizing institutions of family, church, state, and society. But Rousseau turned this settled notion around. He insisted that human nature is at its best prior to and apart from social institutions; that people are naturally loving, virtuous, and selfless; and that it is society, with its artificial rules and conventions, that makes them envious, hypocritical, and competitive.

Rousseau's notion that civilization is artificial is perhaps less surprising when you realize that the society he lived in was just that. Picture the French aristocracy of the 1700s. Women concealed themselves beneath powdered wigs, pasty white makeup, and ornate dresses dripping with jewels and ribbons. Men pranced about in long, curly, powdered wigs; silk waistcoats and frilly cuffs; satin britches; clocked hose; and high-heeled, buckled shoes. Rousseau fled this powdered and polished society, denouncing it as false to the core, and he retreated to small country houses where he could be close to nature. He dressed in shabby, threadbare clothing, but he also delighted in shocking people by wearing bizarre flowing robes and caftans. He refused to practice accepted manners or social formalities, cultivating instead an intensely emotional and spontaneous style of behavior. He kissed his friends ostentatiously, often throwing himself around their necks. He enjoyed playing the part of the tactless, vulgar oaf.

Rousseau's odd dress and crude manners were a deliberate expression of his philosophy: If human nature is essentially good, if evil and corruption are created by a false and hypocritical society, then throw off the restraints of civilization and explore your natural, spontaneous self—the true self that underlies social forms. Free it from stultifying pressures to conform.

These same ideas appear in Rousseau's formal writing on philosophy. He rejected anything that limits the freedom of the inner self, which he saw as naturally good—or, at least, unformed and undefined and capable of being *made* good. Individuals must be free to create themselves by their own choices, free to discover their own identity, free to follow their own road (to quote a Saab advertisement from the mid-nineties). Rousseau's most influential work, *The Social Contract,* opens with the famous line, "Man is born free, and everywhere he is in chains."[5] He called on reformers to set people free from the chains of institutions, rules, customs, and traditions.

Yet ironically Rousseau's philosophy of radical and unbounded freedom spawned the most oppressive regimes of the modern world, inspiring revolutionaries like Robespierre, Marx, Lenin, Hitler, and Mao. Even Pol Pot and his cadre of Paris-educated terrorists were known to have studied Rousseau while their henchmen were slaughtering a quarter of the Cambodian population. How did this happen?

The key is that Rousseau did not define freedom as the assertion of rights against the state; <u>freedom meant liberation from the forms and institutions of *society*—family, church, class, and local community.</u> The state, in fact, would be the liberator. By destroying all social ties, the state would release the individual from loyalty to anything except itself. "Each citizen would then be completely independent of all his fellow men," proclaimed Rousseau, "and absolutely dependent on the state."[6]

This was the first time that the state was actually portrayed as a liberator. For Rousseau, the state "is the agency of emancipation that permits the individual to develop the latent germs of goodness heretofore frustrated by a hostile society."[7] And so was born what one historian calls "the politics of redemption," the idea that politics can be the means not only of creating a better world but of actually transforming human nature, creating "the New Man."[8]

Moreover, since human nature is essentially undefined, according to Rousseau, there are no moral principles limiting the state's ambitions. In the Christian worldview, we treat a thing according to its nature, the type of being it is, based ultimately on what God created it to be. That's why we treat a child differently from a dog. But <u>if there is no such thing as human nature, then there is no justification for saying we should treat people one way rather than another.</u> There is no basis for saying the state must treat its citizens justly instead of unjustly, and there are no moral limitations on the state's use of power.

THE TRAGIC PARADOX

This explains why Rousseau's philosophy gave birth to the modern concept of revolution, which involves not just political rebellion to overthrow a particular ruler but also the wholesale destruction of an existing society in order to build a new, ideal society from scratch. Whereas traditional social theory justified any given action by an appeal to the past—to the normative human nature created by God—modern revolutionaries justify their actions by an appeal to the future—to the ideal society they will create. The bloodiest atrocities can be justified by invoking the perfect society that the revolutionaries promise to build on the ashes of the old.[9] Thus modern revolutionaries moved ruthlessly and brutally, slaughtering millions of people.

Why didn't anyone in Rousseau's legions of disciples foresee these disastrous consequences? Why didn't anyone consider that absolute power is sure to corrupt?

Because utopianism creates a peculiar blindness. Believing the individual to be naturally good, Rousseau was confident that the all-powerful state would likewise be good, since in his view the state was simply a merging of individual wills into a "General Will." Rousseau actually believed that the state would always be right, always tending toward the public good—"always constant, unalterable, and pure."[10] And if some recalcitrant individuals failed to agree with the General Will? That merely proved that they had been corrupted and that they must be coerced into seeing that their true liberty lay in conforming to the General Will. As Rousseau put it, the individual must "be forced to be free."[11]

Robespierre, who led the Reign of Terror that overtook the French Revolution in 1793, grasped this logic all too well. He and his fellow Jacobins understood Rousseau's call for "force" to include condemnation and execution of all who opposed the new order, resulting in the imprisonment of 300,000 nobles, priests, and political dissidents, and the deaths of 17,000 citizens within the year. Of course, this was only the beginning of the rivers of blood that would flow from Rousseau's philosophy. For in practice, the utopian program of building a new and perfect society always means killing off those who resist, those who remain committed to the old ways, or those who belong to a class judged to be irredeemably corrupt (the bourgeoisie, the kulaks, the Jews, the Christians).

This same basic pattern can be seen in the philosophy of Karl Marx, whose vision of a perfect society has fueled one failed utopian experiment after another in nations around the globe. The fatal flaw in Marxism's utopian view of the state is once again the denial of the basic Christian teaching of the Fall. If one is to believe there is such a thing as sin, one must believe there is a

God who is the basis of a transcendent and universal standard of goodness. All this Marx denied. For him, religion and morality were nothing but ideologies used to rationalize the economic interests of one class over another. Small wonder that the totalitarian states created by Marxism acknowledged no universal moral principles, no transcendent justice, and no moral limits on their murderous brutality. The party, like the General Will, was always right.

The same denial of sin explains the roots of fascism. In 1964, *Time* magazine was a latecomer in raising the question on its front cover, "Is God Dead?" Back in the nineteenth century, German philosopher Friedrich Nietzsche had already declared the death of God and had etched out what that meant: the death of morality. He dismissed sin as nothing but a ruse invented by a wretched band of "ascetic priest[s]," Old Testament shamans who had achieved a magical hold over men and women by playing the "ravishing music" of guilt in their souls.[12] And he denounced Christian morality as a morality for slaves. Kindness, forgiveness, humility, obedience, self-denial—these were the characteristics of weak, repressed slaves who had rejected the joy of life. To Nietzsche, the biblical ethic was nothing less than a pathology, a life-killing prudery. He looked forward to the evolution of a race of superhumans imbued with an ethic of power. A century later, the Nazis, taking their cue from Nietzsche, tried to create just such a superrace.

It is paradoxical indeed that such horrors flowed from the idealistic-sounding philosophy of innate human goodness. French satirist Anatole France once observed that never have so many been murdered in the name of a doctrine as in the name of the principle that human beings are naturally good.[13] But if we look into the personal lives of the people who established the philosophy, we begin to see the dark flaw at the heart of their "idealism."

LIBERATION FROM PERSONAL OBLIGATIONS

Take Rousseau. Why did he see oppression only in social institutions such as the family? And why did he paint the state as the
great liberator?

Historian Paul Johnson offers an intriguing hypothesis. At the
time Rousseau was writing *The Social Contract*, Johnson explains,
he was struggling with a great personal dilemma. An inveterate
bohemian, Rousseau had drifted from job to job and mistress
to mistress, eventually living with a simple servant girl named
Thérèse.[14] When Thérèse presented Rousseau with a baby, he
was, in his own words, "thrown into the greatest embarrass-
ment."[15] At that time, he was still trying to make his way into
Parisian high society, and an illegitimate child was an awkward
encumbrance.

Friends whispered to Rousseau that unwanted offspring were
customarily sent to a "foundling asylum," and a few days later, a
tiny, blanketed bundle was left on the steps of the local orphanage.
Four more children were born to Thérèse and Rousseau, and each
ended up on the orphanage steps.[16]

Records show that most of the babies placed in this institution
died; the few who survived became beggars. Rousseau was quite
aware of this unhappy fact; he knew he was abandoning his own
children to almost certain death. In several of his books and let-
ters, he even made vigorous attempts to justify his actions.

At first he was defensive, arguing that he could not work in
a house "filled with domestic cares and the noise of children."[17]
Later his stance became positively self-righteous. He insisted he
was merely following the teachings of Plato, who had declared
the state better equipped than parents to raise good citizens.

When Rousseau turned to writing political theory, his personal
excuses seem to be sublimated into general maxims. His ideal
state turns out to be one that liberates its citizens from troubling
personal obligations. In particular, he urged that responsibility for

educating children should be taken away from parents and given to the state. Was there a connection between Rousseau the man, fleeing from the obligations of fatherhood, and Rousseau the political theorist?

Of course, it's risky business to try to read a philosopher's personal motives from his theoretical writings. But we do know that right up to the end of his life, Rousseau struggled with guilt over his children. In his last book, he grieved that he had "lacked the simple courage to bring up a family."[18]

Ideas do not arise from the intellect alone. They reflect our whole personality, our hopes and fears, our longings and regrets. People who follow a particular course of action are inevitably subject to intellectual pressure to find a rationale for it. Theologians call this the "noetic" effect of sin, meaning that sin affects our minds, our thinking processes. The Reformers coined the phrase "total depravity," meaning that our sinful choices distort all aspects of our being, including our theoretical ideas.

Rousseau's story chillingly refutes the contemporary notion that personal morality has no public consequences. The world has paid dearly for Rousseau's personal choices, from the ovens of Auschwitz to the Game Temple of Synanon. And we're still paying today, in ways that are subtle and thus all the more insidious.

DISCUSSION QUESTIONS

CHAPTER 1

1 Why does being implicated in the broken state of creation threaten people?

2 Why is a utopian view of humanity more palpable than a view of original sin?

3 Read aloud Genesis 2:15-17 and Romans 5:12. What restriction was put on Adam and Eve? What was the result of their disobedience?

4 Read aloud Romans 3:9-24. What aspects of life has sin affected? Think of other aspects not mentioned here.

5 In a sentence summarize the view of reality presented in this Romans passage. Does this view of reality make you feel hopeful or despairing? Give reasons for your answer.

CHAPTERS 2–3

6 Early in chapter 3, the Synanon story is summarized: "What really emerged was total dependence on a cultic authority figure." Discuss the problems inherent in Dederich's strategies.

7 Meg did have reservations along the way. Why was it so hard for her to act on them?

8 What "settled notion" did Rousseau turn around? What influence did this have on the meaning of freedom as he defined it?

9 What are the evidences of Rousseau's philosophy in Marxism? In fascism?

10 Identify seeming benefits in seeing "the state" as one's liberator. Identify corresponding risks.

11 Review Paul Johnson's hypothesis about Rousseau's family situation. Discuss this in terms of how a worldview can have

very personal consequences. In what ways does your worldview affect your family?

12 Martin Luther said: "A Christian is a perfectly free lord of all,
subject to none. A Christian is a perfectly dutiful servant of all,
subject to all." Discuss this paradox in relation to the realities
of community life.

13 How will the material you've read change your expectations for
life, especially in the context of community?

ROLE PLAY

Role plays can be "no pressure" ways for participants to practice
explaining the Christian worldview to skeptics. Remember a few
ground rules. Any comments from listeners should be made (and
received) as encouragement, not as personal criticism. "You might
add this point . . ."; "You might smile more and maintain a
friendly tone"; "You might start with a more basic premise. . . ."

Choose one option, depending on the size of your group and the
group dynamics.

1. In front of the whole group, ask two people to volunteer to act
out a conversation between a skeptic and a Christian. The large
group can give constructive feedback. If time allows another
pair can follow.

2. Have all participants pair off. The two people can alternate, each taking the role of a Christian and skeptic.

3. Have people make groups in threes. One person takes the role of a Christian. The second person takes the role of a skeptic. The third is an observer who gives feedback. Alternate roles.

CONVERSATION STARTERS

  a. Assume a neighbor says, "We're all basically good at heart, don't you think?"

  b. Assume a neighbor says, "We all screw up sometimes. If we just learn to accept and like ourselves, well . . . that's the important thing."

If this role play is difficult, don't give up. The information in the rest of the book will provide more information and arguments for a Christian view of sin and redemption.

CLOSING SUMMARY

What is the one thing you want to remember from what you read (or heard or did) in this session?

  Consider sharing this with the group.

DENYING REALITY

*The utopian illusions and senti-
mental aberrations of modern
liberal culture are really all derived
from the basic error of negating
the fact of original sin.*

REINHOLD NIEBUHR

CHAPTER 4

WE'RE ALL
UTOPIANS NOW

As you read, keep the following questions in mind:
- What form does "soft despotism" take in our society?
- What is fundamentally wrong with a purely scientific view of human nature?
- What role do personal and moral responsibility play in a utopian worldview? In a biblical worldview?

When the Berlin Wall came tumbling down, the rejoicing on this side of the Atlantic had an almost smug ring to it. The Western model of democracy had triumphed, once and for all, over the great tyrannies that had dominated so much of the twentieth century. And indeed, the collapse of the communist behemoth was a profoundly significant political event. But what happened to the ideas that created communism in the first place? Have they quietly died as well?

Not at all. In fact, many Americans and other Western people continue to cherish the same utopian myth that produced such bitter fruit in the totalitarian nations: <u>the same assumption that human nature is basically good, the same rejection of transcendent morality as confining and oppressive, the same grandiose dreams of social engineering.</u> And unless we change these basic presuppositions, we are headed down our own path to tyranny in a form the

great French statesman Alexis de Tocqueville called "soft despotism," an oversolicitous nanny state that debilitates its citizens just
as thoroughly, but by coddling them instead of coercing them.[1]

American utopianism traces its ancestry to Rousseau's notion
of human goodness, but it also exhibits a unique technological,
pragmatic cast that is rooted in the scientific revolution and that
appeals to the Yankee, can-do mind-set. Isaac Newton's dramatic
discovery that a single law—the law of gravity—explained a variety of phenomena, both in the heavens and on the earth, led to an
image of the universe as a vast machine, running by natural laws.
Many people began to extend this machine image into every area
of life, including society itself.[2]

In the eighteenth and nineteenth centuries, social thinkers fer-
vently believed that science would not only explain the physical
world but also show us how to order our lives together harmoni-
ously. They searched for some principle that would explain society
in the same way Newton's law of gravity explained motion—a
principle that would reduce society to a unified, law-governed
system. They sought an experimental physics of the soul that
would enable them to craft a science of government and politics
to conquer the age-old plagues of ignorance, oppression, poverty,
and war.

Of course, nowhere has this vision of scientific utopianism
become a reality. And the reason it continually fails is lodged in
the logic of the scientific method itself. If we turn human beings
into objects for scientific study, we implicitly assume that they are
objects to be manipulated and controlled, like scientific variables.
That means we have to deny things like the soul, conscience,
moral reasoning, and moral responsibility. And when we apply
these assumptions to real social problems, we inevitably dehuman-
ize and demoralize people, placing them at the mercy of social
scientists in the employ of the technocratic state. The end result
is not utopia but another form of despotism.

FROM ANIMAL TO MACHINE

This line of logic can be seen clearly in the field of psychology,
beginning in the nineteenth century with Sigmund Freud,
who did more than anyone else to debunk the very notion of
moral responsibility.[3] Freud reduced humans to complex animals, rejecting explanations of behavior couched in "old-
fashioned" theological terms—such as *sin, soul,* and *conscience*—
and substituting scientific terms borrowed from biology, such
as *instincts* and *drives.* In Freud's theory, people are not so
much rational agents as pawns in the grip of unconscious forces
they do not understand and cannot control. A committed Darwinist, Freud proposed an evolutionary scheme in which our
primitive impulses (the id) belong to the oldest, most animal
part of the human brain, while the rational mind (the ego)
is a later development from the more highly evolved cerebral
cortex. Thus, the things that society labels "bad" are not really
evil; they simply reflect the more ancient, animal part of the
brain.

Later psychologists carried the process of reduction even further. Human nature was modeled not on the animal but on the
machine. The earliest book on experimental psychology was
titled *Elements of Psychophysics,* as if psychology were a branch
of physics. Its author, Gustav Fechner, another radical Darwinist, argued that humans are complicated stimulus-response
mechanisms, shaped by forces in their environment.

After Fechner came Ivan Pavlov, whose name is familiar
because of his experiments conditioning dogs to salivate at the
ringing of a bell. Pavlov, an evolutionist and materialist, adamantly rejected any notion of soul, spirit, or even consciousness.
All mental life, he declared (whether in his salivating dogs or in
human beings), could be explained in entirely mechanical terms
of stimulus and response.

In the 1960s, B. F. Skinner's *Walden Two* introduced millions of college students to behaviorism, a school of psychology that flatly denies the reality of consciousness or mental states. Because these things cannot be observed, Skinner argued, they cannot be described scientifically; therefore, they are not real. Only observable, external behavior is real.[4]

By denying the reality of the mind, Skinner and the behaviorists believed they were "purifying" psychology of all philosophical prejudices and rendering it completely scientific and objective. In reality, of course, they were simply injecting their own philosophical prejudices. They were creating a new brand of "scientific" utopianism, which said that the flaws in human nature are a result not of moral corruption but of learned responses— responses that can be *un*learned so that people can then be reprogrammed to be happy and adjusted, living in harmony in a utopian society.

RESULTANT SHIFT IN EDUCATION AND LAW

One of the results of this utopian thinking was a shift in education. Classical education had always aimed at the pursuit of truth and the training of moral character. But if human nature was nothing more than a reactive mechanism, then it could be manipulated and shaped by the laws that science discovered. Thus, education became a means of conditioning, with the child being treated as essentially passive rather than as an active moral agent.

Of course, this dehumanizing philosophy is always presented in the language of utopian promise. In the words of J. B. Watson, the founder of behaviorism, "Give me the baby and . . . the possibility of shaping in any direction is almost endless."[5] Forget trying to reform behavior through religion and morality; these are merely forms of oppression. Through education the world can be "unshackled from legendary folklore . . . free of foolish customs and conventions . . . which hem the individual in like taut steel bands." Watson, sounding eerily like an early Charles Dederich, promised to bring up children with "better ways of living," who "in turn will bring up their children in a still more scientific way, until the world finally becomes a place fit for human habitation."[6]

The same ideas were applied to law. Traditionally in the West, positive law (or human law) was based on a transcendent standard of justice, derived ultimately from God's law. But in the late nineteenth century, legal thinkers like Oliver Wendell Holmes, influenced by Darwin and the rise of social science, began to shift these foundations (as we will see later). They reduced law to a summary of the social and economic policies proven scientifically to work best. The law was redefined as a tool for identifying and manipulating the right factors to create social harmony and progress.

RESULTANT RISE IN WELFARE STATE

The same scientific utopianism explains the rise of the welfare state. The idea that both law and government policy should be transformed into social engineering took root in the New Deal of the 1930s and blossomed in the Great Society programs of the 1960s. Many American politicians became enthusiastic converts, sincerely believing that all it would take to solve the problems of poverty and crime would be some well-designed, well-funded government programs. They were confident they could win President Lyndon Johnson's "war on poverty."

Well, today the war is over, and poverty won. The welfare state has backfired, creating both a near permanent underclass of dependency and a host of attendant social pathologies, from broken families and teen pregnancy to drug abuse and crime. What went wrong?

Novelist Dean Koontz discovered the answer through hard experience. In the 1960s, young, idealistic, and eager to change the world, Koontz signed up as a counselor in Title III of the Appalachian Poverty Program. His job was to work with problem students, giving them one-on-one tutoring and counseling to help them break out of the area's depressed economic situation. But when Koontz showed up for work, he discovered that many of the students had criminal records. In fact, the man who preceded him on the job had been beaten up by the kids he was there to help and had ended up in the hospital. Koontz soon realized these kids needed a lot more than a bit of tutoring. They needed forms of moral guidance and discipline, which they were not getting at home or school. By the end of his first year in the program, a discouraged Koontz realized that the notion of reforming society through government programs was itself misguided. The failed Great Society programs, he writes, are an illustration of "humanity's hopeless pursuit of utopia through government beneficence."[7]

Koontz puts his finger squarely on the problem: the "hopeless pursuit of utopia." The utopianism of the Great Society offered no real answer to the dilemma of moral breakdown—to crime and social disorder—because it redefined moral maladies as technical problems that could be solved by bureaucrats. Instead of treating human beings as moral agents who must be addressed in the language of duty and responsibility, the Great Society treated them as objects to be shaped and manipulated. As a result, its programs tended to undercut the moral dignity of their recipients, leaving millions dependent and demoralized.

Again we see the irony: When we deny the Christian worldview and reject its teachings on sin and moral responsibility in favor of a more "enlightened" and "scientific" view of human nature, we actually end up stripping people of their dignity and treating them as less than human.

Public Housing

Public housing is another example. In the 1920s, progressives began clearing city slums and replacing them with housing projects built to hygienic and sociological standards. These great, hulking structures reflected the utilitarian, technocratic vision. They were drab, stark towers of steel and concrete, impersonal and functional, designed to warehouse as many people as possible, as efficiently as possible.

The results? Walls that belonged to no one were soon defaced by graffiti. Hallways that belonged to no one were soon stalked by criminals and drug dealers. Grounds that no one was responsible for were soon dry, dusty, and littered with junk. The housing projects designed with such scientific care turned into seedbeds of crime and misery.

Many of these projects have even had to be demolished. When a housing project in Newark, New Jersey, was dynamited, former residents stood by cheering. By contrast, the city mayor mourned "the end of an American dream that failed."[8]

Yet the dream has *not* died. As housing projects collapse into rubble, plans for new social engineering schemes are on the drafting table. And these, too, will fail. Why? Because the source of the welfare-state crisis is not a few wrongheaded policies; it's the utopian philosophy behind the policies—a worldview that regards human beings as ciphers that can be molded and manipulated, tinkered with and retooled, to fit the visions of social planners.

Beyond Freedom and Dignity

The trouble with the technocratic vision is that it reduces individuals to passive recipients of the state's ministrations, thus robbing them of liberty and initiative. Small wonder that B. F. Skinner's vision of a technocratic utopia was set out in a book called *Beyond Freedom and Dignity*. The title pressed the point that the only way

to force people to fit into any ideal blueprint for society is to
jettison traditional notions of human freedom and dignity.

Entitlement Mentality

Moreover, when things go wrong, when poverty and crime prove
intractable, the assumption is that the state is not doing enough.
Thus we have bred an entitlement mentality wherein people
believe that government owes them support even if they do not
fulfill the basic duties of citizenship—or even if they engage in
harmful or illegal behavior.

Do they use drugs? Are they alcoholics? Are they able-
bodied but refuse to work? Are they having children without
the slightest intention of supporting them? No matter. They
are entitled to government benefits, no questions asked. Thus
these dysfunctional patterns are reinforced, and the cycle continues. Citizens are offered no encouragement to assume moral
or personal responsibility for their lives. It's no surprise, then,
that welfare has spawned an underclass in which dysfunctional
and illegal behavior is the norm. By ignoring the moral dimension, by reducing social disorders to technical problems to be
addressed with scientific solutions, we have created moral
chaos.

Scientific utopianism always backfires. It expands government
control while gradually sapping citizens of moral responsibility,
economic initiative, and personal prudence.

A MATTER OF THE SOUL

But welfare is not the only area of public policy that illustrates the
pernicious effects of the utopian myth. When it comes to crime,
America's criminal justice policy swings back and forth between
liberal and conservative approaches: from an emphasis on rehabil-
itation and social engineering to an emphasis on tougher laws and

harsher sentences. Yet both approaches exemplify, in different ways, the same utopian worldview.

Traditional Liberal Approach

Traditional liberalism fixes responsibility for crime on poverty and other social ills. Crime is not a matter of the soul, says the liberal; it is a technical problem that can be solved by engineering the right social conditions: devising the right public policies, distributing money to the right places, and arranging the right physical environment. This view was expressed at the dawn of the Great Society by then Attorney General Ramsey Clark. He enumerated the causes of crime in sordid detail: "the dehumanizing effect on the individual of slums, racism, ignorance and violence, of corruption and impotence to fulfill rights, of poverty and unemployment and idleness, of generations of malnutrition, of congenital brain damage and prenatal neglect, of sickness and disease, of pollution, of decrepit, dirty, ugly, unsafe, overcrowded housing, of alcoholism and narcotics addiction, of avarice, anxiety, fear, hatred, hopelessness and injustice."

Astonishingly, after reciting this horrendous litany, Clark concluded optimistically: "They can be controlled." Never mind how universal, how endemic, how intractable these problems are; they are all merely technical malfunctions that can be fixed by applying the right technical solution.[9]

Furthermore, since liberalism regards crime as the outcome of impersonal forces in society, it locates responsibility for crime outside the criminal. Already at the turn of the century, Clarence Darrow, the lawyer who achieved notoriety defending Darwinism in the Scopes trial, was portraying criminals as helpless victims of their circumstances. In 1902, in a widely published speech to the prisoners in Chicago's Cook County Jail, he declared that "there is no such thing as a crime as the word is generally understood. . . . I do not believe that people are in jail because they deserve to be.

They are in jail simply because they cannot avoid it on account of circumstances which are entirely beyond their control and for which they are in no way responsible."[10]

Today, Darrow's heirs fill courtrooms across the country, wringing pity from juries by presenting wrongdoers as victims of forces beyond their control. This kind of defense has grown so common that it is now known as the "Twinkie defense," named for a 1978 case in which a man pleaded temporary insanity after shooting the mayor and the city supervisor in San Francisco's city hall. He insisted that a steady diet of junk food had raised his blood sugar and addled his brain. Twinkies made him do it.

While this liberal approach is often presented as caring and compassionate, the truth is that it is based on a low view of human nature. As Myron Magnet writes in *The Dream and the Nightmare,* liberalism treats people as passive products of the environment, like corn or alfalfa, that automatically grow or wilt depending on the rain and sunshine.[11]

Traditional Conservative Approach

Yet the traditional conservative approach is equally dehumanizing, for it treats crime as little more than a calculation of incentives. It proposes that crime increases when the benefits of criminal behavior outweigh the cost of punishment. Therefore, the solution is harsher punishments and longer sentences. I know this approach intimately, having written many of President Nixon's law-and-order slogans when I was in the White House. How we curried applause in conservative circles with that tough rhetoric!

Ultimately this approach stems from a mechanistic philosophy that reduces the world to mathematical relations and truth to calculation. It treats people not as moral agents who are disposed to sin but as complex calculating machines that total up incentives, weigh them against disincentives, and then decide whether to commit a crime.

Double Failure

America's staggering crime rate from the 1960s through the 1980s demonstrates that both liberal and conservative approaches to criminal justice have failed. Why? Because neither recognizes the dignity of the soul and its ability to make morally significant choices. Neither respects human beings as genuine moral agents, capable of both real good and real evil. And neither addresses the need for moral responsibility and repentance.

Age of Exoneration

This denial of sin and loss of moral responsibility has spread across the entire spectrum of our culture, ushering in "The Golden Age of Exoneration."[12] When people are consistently told that they are controlled by outside forces, they begin to believe it. When things go wrong, someone else must be to blame.

Preposterous examples are legion. Like the woman who entered a hot-dog-eating contest in a Houston nightclub. In her rush to outdo the other contestants, she ate too quickly and began to choke. Did the woman shrug off the mishap as a natural consequence of her own zany behavior? No, she decided she was a victim. She sued the nightclub that sponsored the contest, arguing that the business was to blame because "they shouldn't have contests like that."[13]

The victim ploy can be attractive because it frees us from having to admit to wrongdoing. Yet it is in admitting guilt that we find our true dignity, for doing so affirms the moral dimension of human nature. For centuries, Western law codes and social morality were based on a high regard for individual responsibility. It was understood that human beings are moral agents capable of distinguishing right from wrong, and are, therefore, accountable for their actions.

Of course, acknowledging responsibility means attributing real praise and blame—and blame, in turn, implies the legitimacy of punishment. That's what makes moral accountability so bittersweet. Yet punishment actually expresses a high view of the human being. If a person who breaks the law is merely a dysfunctional victim of circumstances, then the remedy is not justice but therapy; and the lawbreaker is not a person with rights but a patient to be cured. The problem, said C. S. Lewis, is that "to be 'cured' against one's will . . . is to be put on a level with those who have not yet reached the age of reason or those who never will; to be classed with infants, imbeciles, and domestic animals. But to be punished, however severely, because we have deserved it, because we 'ought to have known better,' is to be treated as a human person made in God's image."[14]

"OF ALL TYRANTS"

Denial of sin may appear to be a benign and comforting doctrine, but in the end, it is demeaning and destructive, for it denies the significance of our choices and actions. It reduces us to pawns in the grip of larger forces: either unconscious forces in the human psyche or economic and social forces in the environment. Social planners and controllers then feel perfectly justified in trying to control those forces, to remake human nature and rebuild society according to their own blueprints—and to apply any force required toward that end.

"Of all tyrannies a tyranny sincerely exercised for the good of its victims may be the most oppressive," wrote Lewis. "Those who torment us for our own good will torment us without end for they do so with the approval of their own conscience."[15]

Utopianism can be maintained only by a kind of willful blindness to the reality of human sin. But when we succumb to that blindness, we lose the capacity to deal with sin, and in the end, we actually compound its effects. Therein lies the greatest paradox of all attempts to deny the Fall: <u>In denying sin and evil, we actually unleash its worst powers.</u>

*Sin cannot be overcome by human
devices of the kind that govern-
ments wield but only by suffering
and by grace.*   GLENN TINDER

CHAPTER 5

THE FACE OF EVIL

As you read, keep the following questions in mind:

- How and why is the face of evil "frighteningly ordinary"?
- What is the popular culture's attitude toward sin?
- What has replaced a "vocabulary of moral responsibility" and why?
- What happens when a worldview that is "too small" denies reality? How is this evident in our society?

What does the face of evil look like?

A few years ago when I visited a South Carolina women's prison, I learned that Susan Smith had signed up to hear me speak. Smith is the woman who drowned her two small sons by letting her car slide into a lake with the children still strapped in their car seats. Her reason? She felt that the man she was dating had hinted that the children were obstacles to marrying her.

As I prepared to speak that day, I scanned the audience, wondering what this unnatural mother would look like. I imagined some kind of female Dorian Gray, her face marked by the soul-struggle she had waged with evil. Recalling photos from the newspaper, I searched for her face, but I couldn't pick her out.

After the meeting, I asked the local Prison Fellowship director whether Smith had even attended. "Oh, sure," he replied. "She was in the front row, staring at you the whole time."

<u>The face of evil is frighteningly ordinary.</u>

In Jonesboro, Arkansas, an eleven- and a thirteen-year-old pull the school fire alarm, assume sniper positions, and then shoot at students and teachers as they file out of the school. They kill four students and one teacher, wounding eleven others.[1]

In Oakland, California, a teenager with a knife chases a woman down the street, while a crowd gathers and chants, "Kill her! Kill her!" like spectators at a sporting event. Someone in the crowd finally trips the frightened woman, giving her assailant a chance to stab her to death.[2]

In Dartmouth, Massachusetts, three boys surround a ninth-grade classmate and stab him to death. Afterward they laugh and trade high fives, like basketball players celebrating after a slam dunk.[3]

In New Jersey, Brian Peterson takes his girlfriend, Amy Grossberg, across the state line to a Delaware hotel room, where she gives birth. They kill the newborn and dump him in the trash.[4]

Killers with freckled faces. Killers on the playground. Killers who do it for sport.

What does the face of evil look like? It looks like the kid next door. It looks like us.

How can we view this carnage, this unspeakable evil lurking behind the wholesome grin of an eleven-year-old, and still cling to the myth that humans are basically good?

THE PROBLEM IS . . .

Media coverage of these heinous crimes offered all the conventional answers. The problem is poverty. (But most of these killers were middle class.) The problem is race—for there is a hushed racism in much of our perception of crime. (But most of these perpetrators were white.) The problem is a dysfunctional childhood—the therapeutic catchphrase these days for all abnormal behavior. (But millions of kids come from harsh circumstances and never commit a crime.)

The only explanation not offered is the one that modern commentators cannot bring themselves to utter: the dreaded "s word". . . *sin.* It is sin that unleashes the capacity for raw evil. It is sin that blinds us to anything beyond our own selfish desires. As the judge said to Amy Grossberg during her sentencing, "If there is a disturbing aspect to your character, . . . it was an egocentricity that blinded you to the need to seek help, and to the intrinsic value of the life of the child."[5]

Sin is choosing what we know is wrong. After he had interviewed Susan Smith's pastor, a reporter for the *New York Times Magazine* concluded with this analysis: Smith "had a choice between good and evil. She had a choice and knew what she was doing when she made it."[6] How rarely we hear people acknowledge this stark, simple truth. We have a choice, and when we sin, we choose to do evil.

TEACH YOUR CHILDREN WELL

How have we lost touch with such a fundamental truth? To begin with, look at the way children are raised today. A generation ago, children and adolescents were still subject to moral discipline at school, following a long-standing tradition that regarded moral character as important as academic ability. Teachers believed that part of their role was to encourage virtue and instill restraints against the ever threatening lure of sin and immorality. This tradition dates back to colonial days when little girls in aprons and little boys in knee britches learned how to read from *The New England Primer,* which taught the alphabet along with almost gloomy theological lessons.

A—In Adam's fall,
   we sinned all. . . .
I—The idle fool
   is whipt at school. . . .
X—Xerxes did die,
   and so must I.[7]

How different from the modern classroom, where children are
taught, above all else, to like themselves. Where even grammatical
errors go uncorrected lest a red mark damage the student's self-
esteem. Where "guilt" is something hazardous to mental well-
being, an artificial constraint from which we need to be liberated.
As a result, <u>today's younger generation does not even understand
the vocabulary of moral responsibility.</u> Is it surprising, then, that
we now see kids who show no remorse when they violate the
rights of others, from trivial things like stealing a sister's blouse
to horrific crimes like gunning down a classmate?

The utopian myth has even taken hold in the home, where the
same ideas are served up through magazines, parenting seminars,
maternity classes, and books on child development. Back in the
1940s, in the most influential book ever written for parents, Dr.
Benjamin Spock encouraged parents to reject the old puritan
notion of children as savages, prone to evil and in need of civilizing. Instead, he urged them to understand children as evolving
psyches in need of attention. For example, when a school-age
child steals something, Spock suggests that parents consider
whether their child might "need more . . . approval at home," and
even a raise in his allowance![8]

The same message was advanced in the most popular parenting
books of the 1960s and 1970s: Haim Ginott's *Between Parent and
Child* and Thomas Gordon's *Parent Effectiveness Training*. These
books aimed at transforming parents from stern moralizers into
sympathetic therapists, who were to remain coolheaded,

nonjudgmental, even professional in their demeanor, calmly leading their children to "clarify" their own values.[9]

Thus, even in the home, the heart and hearth of society, a
sense of duty has been replaced by a sense of entitlement, a sense
that we have a right to what we want, even if it means violating
standards of proper behavior. Adults who once gave firm and
unequivocal moral direction—parents, teachers, even pastors—
have been indoctrinated with the idea that the way to ensure
healthy children is not to tell them what's right and wrong but to
let them discover their own values. As a result, many Americans
have lost even the vocabulary of moral accountability. Sin and
moral responsibility have become alien concepts.[10]

Just how deeply this has affected us was evident in an MTV
network special news report on "The Seven Deadly Sins," which
aired in August 1993. A description of the program looked
promising enough—interviews with celebrities and ordinary
teens talking about the seven deadly sins: lust, pride, anger, envy,
sloth, greed, and gluttony. But what came across most forcefully
was the participants' shocking moral ignorance.

Rap star Ice-T glared into the camera and growled, "Lust isn't
a sin. . . . These are all dumb."

One young man on the street seemed to think sloth was a work
break. "Sloth. . . . Sometimes it's good to sit back and give yourself
personal time."

Pride was the sin the MTV generation found hardest to grasp.
"Pride isn't a sin—you're supposed to feel good about yourself,"
one teen said. Actress Kirstie Alley agreed. "I don't think pride
is a sin, and I think some idiot made that up," she snapped.

The program offered not one word about guilt, repentance,
or moral responsibility. Instead, it was littered with psychothera-
peutic jargon, as if sin were a sickness or addiction. Even the
program narrator joined the chorus: "The seven deadly sins are
not evil acts, but rather universal human compulsions."[11]

BEYOND JARGON

The utopian mind-set has become so pervasive that most people in Western culture have no intellectual resources to identify or deal with genuine wrongdoing. For example, when a respected historian wrote a book about mass murderers like Hitler and Stalin, all he could say was that they were subject to "mental disorders."[12] Every one of us is affected by this degeneration of moral discourse, to the point where even Christians are prone to use the vocabulary of therapy instead of the sterner language of morality.

The question of genuine evil was posed with brutal honesty in Thomas Harris's *The Silence of the Lambs,* a horror novel made into a grisly but riveting movie. In it, an imprisoned serial killer named Hannibal Lecter, a monster who cannibalizes his victims, is approached by a young female FBI agent who hopes he can give her information that will help catch another brutal killer.

"What possible reason could I have for cooperating with you?" asks Lecter.

"Curiosity," says Officer Starling.

"About what?"

"About why you're here. About what happened to you."

"Nothing happened to me, Officer Starling. *I* happened. You can't reduce me to a set of influences. You've given up good and evil for behaviorism, Officer Starling. . . . Nothing is ever anybody's fault. Look at me, Officer Starling. Can you say I'm evil? Am I evil, Officer Starling?"[13]

Hannibal Lecter's taunting question blows away the accumulated jargon that clogs our brains. We do know, both intuitively and from experience, that evil is real. We sense a force—in ourselves and in others—that has the power to dominate and destroy.

REALITY CHECK

The fatal flaw in the myth of human goodness is that it fails to correspond with what we know about the world from our own ordinary experience. And when a worldview is too small, when it denies the existence of some part of reality, that part will reassert itself in some way, demanding our attention. It's like trying to squeeze a balloon in your hands: Some parts will always bulge out. Our sense of sin will always find expression in some form.

Take, for example, the enormous appetite Americans have for horror fiction. What explains this fascination? Part of the answer is that these books deal with gnawing questions about the depth of human evil. This may be one reason Stephen King's novels top the charts again and again. For in King's gruesome world, evil is threateningly real, and supernatural forces lurk everywhere, seeking whom they may devour. Normal people are drawn to these grim stories for the same reason a small child wants to hear the story of the "Three Little Pigs" over and over again, each time delighting in the way the resourceful third pig heats a pot of boiling water in his fireplace to scald the big bad wolf when he sneaks down the chimney.

Children love fairy tales, especially the classic ones recorded by the Brothers Grimm, because they're stocked with scary villains—evil stepmothers and wicked witches, ugly trolls and fierce dragons. Children instinctively know that evil exists, and they gravitate toward stories that symbolize the bad and scary things of life through fantasy characters—and then show those characters being soundly defeated by the good.

Psychologist Bruno Bettelheim says well-meaning parents who refuse to read these spine-tingling stories to their children are not doing the kids a favor. Instead, they're denying them a chance to face their very real fears within the safely sheltered realm of fantasy—in a story where the witches and goblins disappear with the words "happily ever after."[14]

For adults, fiction can provide a similar function: a way of confronting the dark side of reality. Novelist Susan Wise Bauer says adults living in a world of tragedy and pain "need a Grimm for grown-ups—a narrative that not only explains the presence of evil but offers a triumph over it."[15]

Horror/thriller writer Dean Koontz believes the popularity of his own novels about serial killers stems from readers' hunger for pictures of the world painted in vivid moral hues. In our therapeutic age, we have been taught that "one form of behavior is as valid as another," that even murder and destruction must not be condemned but understood, Koontz says. "In 'enlightened' thought there is no true evil." But in our daily life, we know this isn't true. This explains why "people gravitate to fiction that says there is true evil, that there is a way to live that is good, and that there is a way to live that is bad. And that these are moral choices." People have an "inner need to see what they really know on a gut level about life reflected in the entertainment they view or the literature they read."[16]

In a world where juries excuse the inexcusable, where psychologists explain away the most inexplicable evils, people are groping for a kind of realism that they find, ironically, in fiction.

WHEN WE CANNOT NAME EVIL . . .

The fact is that a utopian framework has taken away the conceptual tools we need to grapple effectively with genuine evil. And when we cannot name or identify evil, we lose the capacity to deal with it—and ultimately we compound its deadly effects.

I saw this in a tragic way a few years ago during a visit to Norway. The prisons there resemble the snow-draped landscape: cold and white. Officials are proud of their prison system, with its expensive, up-to-date facilities. They brag that, along with the Swedes, they employ the most humane and progressive methods of treatment anywhere in the world, and many penologists agree.

The prison I visited just outside of Oslo was a model maximum-security facility. I was greeted by the warden, a psychiatrist with a clinically detached attitude. As she showed me through the sterile surroundings, which seemed more like a laboratory than a prison, she touted the number of counselors and the types of therapies given to inmates. In fact, we met so many other psychiatrists that I asked the warden how many of the inmates were mental cases.

"All of them, of course," she replied quickly, raising her eyebrows in surprise.

"What do you mean, 'all of them'?"

"Well, anyone who commits a violent crime is obviously mentally unbalanced."

Ah, yes. People are basically good, so anyone who could do something so terrible must be mentally ill. And the solution is therapy. I was seeing the therapeutic model fully realized. Tragically, I would also soon see its failure.

That day I spoke to an audience of inmates. Typically, prison is the one place where I don't have to belabor the message of sin; it's one biblical truth that men and women behind bars know well. But these inmates remained completely unmoved by anything I said, even the invitation to receive Christ. No response. Only glazed expressions.

As I was leaving, however, I was approached by an attractive young correctional officer who identified herself as a Christian. In perfect English she thanked me, then said, "I've prayed for this day, when these men would be confronted with a solid message of sin and salvation." She went on to describe her frustration at having to work within such a flawed system, where there was no concept of personal responsibility, and therefore no reason to seek personal transformation.

Only days later, her criticisms of the system were horribly borne out. By then, I had traveled on to Scotland, and while there, I received an urgent phone call from the Norwegian Prison Fellowship workers. They soberly informed me that the young officer I had met had been given the responsibility of escorting an inmate out to see a movie—part of the inmate's therapy—and on the way back, he had overpowered her, raped her, and then murdered her.

A sign of mental illness? A result of social or economic forces? How pale and ineffective such explanations appear beside the monstrosity of human cruelty and violence. <u>When we embrace nonmoral categories to explain away moral evil, we fail to take it seriously, and we fail to constrain it.</u> When we refuse to listen to the true diagnosis of the sickness of the soul, we will not find a true remedy, and in the end it will destroy us.

TWO RESTRAINTS

In any society, only two forces hold the sinful nature in check: the restraint of conscience or the restraint of the sword. The less that citizens have of the former, the more the state must employ the latter. A society that fails to keep order by an appeal to civic duty and moral responsibility must resort to coercion—either open coercion, as practiced by totalitarian states, or covert coercion, where citizens are wooed into voluntarily giving up their freedom. Given the examples cited at the beginning of this chapter, it's not much of a stretch to imagine Americans eventually so frightened of their own children that they will welcome protection by ever greater government control. That's why utopianism always leads to the loss of liberty.

The only alternative to increased state control is a return to biblical realism about the human potential for evil, a bracing

willingness to look evil in the eye and not flinch. Sociologists
are constantly searching for the root causes of crime and other
dysfunctions in society. But the root cause has not changed since
the temptation in the Garden. It is sin.

Human beings have revolted against God and his created order,
throwing the entire creation out of joint. Everything is distorted
by sin. Nothing is free from its effects. This is not merely a "religious" message, limited to some "private" realm of faith. It is the
truth about ultimate reality. And as we examine that truth more
closely, we will see clearly why the biblical worldview provides the
only rational basis for living in the real world.

DISCUSSION QUESTIONS

CHAPTER 4

1 What dehumanizing evidences do you see resulting from a "soft despotism" of scientific utopianism?

2 Read aloud Genesis 3:1-6. To Eve, what was the appeal of the forbidden fruit? By disobeying, who was Eve putting at the center of her world (and worldview)?

3 Read aloud Genesis 3:7-19. What effects of sin are described here? (See vv. 7, 8, 12, 16, 17-19.) Give examples of how the "reality" portrayed in Genesis 3 does or does not jibe with your own experience.

4 What is the appeal of reducing human nature to a "machine model"? How does this model compare with the biblical model of humans being made in the image of God?

5   Even for Christians, what is the appeal of "easy answers" to difficult questions? Have you ever tried to "reduce the world to mathematical relations and the truth to calculation"? How and why?

6   Compare and contrast an "entitlement mentality" and a "victim mentality" with a biblical mentality grounded in personal responsibility.

CHAPTER 5

7   What words would you include in a "vocabulary list" of moral responsibility? (Have someone in the group write down the words, if possible, on a large board or flip chart.)

8   What words would you include in a "vocabulary list" of therapeutic jargon? (Have someone in the group write down the words, if possible, on a large board or flip chart.)

9   Have someone read aloud your moral responsibility list. Listen with the ears of your secular neighbors and friends. What do you think they're hearing? How will this exercise influence the way you use these words in conversation?

10 As an object lesson showing that "our sense of sin will always find expression in some form," have someone blow up a balloon (not so tight that it might pop). Squeeze the balloon at one end or in the middle. Discuss the exaggerated ways in which people react to the culture's denial of evil.

11 In what healthy ways can you help your children—and yourself—recognize the existence and the pervasiveness of evil?

12 How will the material you've read in chapters 1–5 change your attitude toward and the way you treat other people, marred by sin but made in the image of God?

13 How will the material you've read in chapters 1–5 change your awareness of taking personal responsibility for yourself, your actions, and your family?

ROLE PLAY

Refer to the directions for role play at the end of session 1 (pp. 40–41).

CONVERSATION STARTER

Stage a devil-on-your-shoulder-type conversation. Assume that you have done something wrong, maybe stolen your neighbor's rake or told a lie about a coworker so you will not be blamed for a mistake you made. Have a conversation that might go on inside your own head, between the part of you that knows you should admit your guilt and the part of you that is justifying what you've done (think in terms of what you've learned about an entitlement mentality, a victim mentality, and therapeutic jargon).

CLOSING SUMMARY
What is the one thing you want to remember from what you read (or heard or did) in this session?

Consider sharing this with the group.

SIN, SUFFERING, AND THE FACT OF FREEDOM

CHAPTER 6

A SNAKE IN THE GARDEN

As you read, keep the following questions in mind:
- What is the original "Great Lie"?
- What was the original sin?
- What is the biblical view of sin, and what makes it unique?
- What "intolerable dilemma" do nonbelievers face?

The best diagnosis of the human condition is "all in the first few pages of Genesis," says theologian Nigel Cameron.[1] In those pages we learn where we came from, what our purpose is, and what has gone wrong with the world.

When God created the first two human beings, Adam and Eve, he set a moral limit: "You are free to eat from any tree in the garden; but you must not eat from the tree of the knowledge of good and evil, for when you eat of it you will surely die" (Gen. 2:16-17). Adam and Eve were free either to believe God and obey his law or to disobey him and suffer the consequences. This same choice has confronted every person throughout history.

Obedience to God is not just a matter of following rules arbitrarily imposed by a harsh master. Obedience to God is a means of entering into real life, a life rich in meaning and purpose: "See, I set before you today life and prosperity, death and destruction. . . . Now choose life, so that you and your children may live" (Deut. 30:15, 19).

And obedience is not simply about external acts. Obedience is an internal response to God as a personal being; it is choosing to know and "love the Lord your God with all your heart and with all your soul and with all your strength" (Deut. 6:5). At the core of God's commandments is not a set of principles or a list of expectations; at the heart of God's commandments is a *relationship*. We are to love God with our whole being.

To create personal beings capable of this kind of relationship, however, God had to create beings capable of choice. These were not human puppets dangling from celestial strings but morally significant agents who are capable of altering the course of history by the choices they make.

This does not imply that the Bible endorses the contemporary notion of autonomous "choice," where whatever I choose becomes right for me by virtue of the fact that I choose it. The Bible teaches that there is a holy God whose law constitutes a transcendent, universally valid standard of right and wrong. Our choice has no effect at all on this standard; <u>our choice simply determines whether we accept it, or reject it and suffer the consequences.</u>

THE ENTRANCE OF EVIL

God is good, and his original creation was good. God is not the author of evil. This is a crucial element in Christian teaching, for if God had created evil, then his own essence would contain both good and evil, and there would be no hope that good could ever triumph over evil.[2] There would be no basis for any doctrine of salvation, for God could not save us from evil if the same evil were lodged in his own nature. There also would be no basis for fighting against injustice and oppression, against cruelty and corruption, for these, too, would be reflections of God's own nature and, therefore, inherent in the world as he created it.

The biblical teaching of the original goodness of creation solves two important philosophical problems: It explains the source of evil, and it grounds our hope of personal salvation. If we had been created with a fatal flaw, then salvation would require destroying us and starting over. But since we were created good, salvation means restoring us to what we were originally created to be. Redemption means the restoration and fulfillment of God's original purposes.

But if God is good and creation is good, what is the ultimate origin of evil? Again we turn to the early pages of Genesis, where we are told about the temptation of Eve by a powerful spiritual being who appeared in the form of a serpent and insinuated his destructive ideas simply by raising questions. "Did God really say, 'You must not eat from any tree in the garden'?" the serpent asked (Gen. 3:1). Then, having raised doubts, he moved in for the kill, issuing a direct contradiction to the divine word. The serpent boldly announced: "You will not surely die" (Gen. 3:4). He blatantly confronted the truth with a lie.

And where did this serpent—this evil being—come from? Throughout history, all cultures have had some concept of evil as a real entity, some force personified as a devil or an evil god— or what philosophers call "presence." Only in the Bible do we learn the true source of this evil force. There is an invisible realm of spiritual beings, both good angels and fallen ones (demons), and there is a moral battle going on in this invisible world, just as there is in the visible world. Occasionally Scripture pulls aside the curtain to give us a brief glimpse of that invisible battle.

One of the main characters in this battle is a fallen angel, a once-perfect being who made a moral decision to rebel against God. This being is called "the accuser" or "Satan" or "the devil."[3] In the first chapter of the Old Testament book of Job, Satan boasts that he goes freely "roaming through the earth and going back and forth in it" in his search for souls to corrupt (Job 1:7).

Thousands of years later, the apostle Peter, apparently picking up this image from Job, warns that the devil "prowls around like a roaring lion looking for someone to devour" (1 Pet. 5:8). In the Gospels, we learn that after Judas made his fateful decision to betray Jesus, "Satan entered into him" (John 13:27), a hair-raising phrase that tells us an evil spirit can extend its grip deep into a person's soul once that person has made the decision to betray the Lord. Jesus warned that Satan's primary mode of operation is deceit: "He is a liar and the father of lies" (John 8:44).

Satan's own fall from grace began when he declared his intention to be like God: "I will make myself like the Most High" (Isa. 14:14). He then enticed Eve with the same temptation: If you eat from the tree, you will be like the Most High, able to determine good and evil. As Francis Schaeffer puts it, Satan is "the originator of The Great Lie"—that we have the capacity, like God, to create our own standard of right and wrong.[4] It is a lie repeated so often that it has become the accepted wisdom of our culture.

We can almost imagine the crowds of angels, knowing that all of human history hangs in the balance, watching in tense silence as Satan makes his offer to Eve. And we can almost hear then the collective groan of sorrow as Eve reaches out her hand and grasps the fruit. She has believed the lie!

"She also gave some [of the fruit] to her husband, who was with her, and he ate it" (Gen. 3:6). In these utterly simple words lies the explanation for the human dilemma that has bowed generations upon generations under a load of suffering and pain. Adam and Eve's sin was not eating a piece of fruit. Their sin was coveting godlike power, craving something that was not rightfully theirs. They rejected their nature as created, limited, finite beings, and they tried to be what they could never be— divine. They wanted to be their own god.

SIN AFFECTS ALL

This single choice to disobey a divine command introduced the moral battle of the heavenlies into the earthly arena, with consequences that will reach to the end of history. The original sin in the Garden has affected all of humanity, so that every human being is born into a state of alienation from God.

A young convert once asked Nancy, "Aren't Adam and Eve just symbols for all humanity, and isn't the Fall merely a symbol of the sin that traps us all?" No, this is not a mythical fable. These were real choices, made by real human beings. As the apostle Paul declares again and again in Romans 5, Adam and Eve's fall into sin was as historical as Christ's redemptive work on Calvary. And the reverse holds as well: Because the Fall was genuinely historical, the second person of the Trinity had to enter history and suffer a historical death and resurrection to bring about redemption.

The biblical explanation of evil is not some intellectual exercise or a theoretical way to explain what's wrong with the world. Instead, it carries an unavoidable personal message: that *each of us* has sinned against a holy God. As the apostle Paul writes, "There is no one righteous, not even one. . . . All have turned away" (Rom. 3:10-12). When we truly understand these words, we are gripped by a profound humility. We realize that we all come into this world on an equal moral standing before God; we all need the redemption that God alone can provide.

Virtually every other worldview draws the line separating good and evil between sets of people: between Jew and Gentile, between Aryan and non-Aryan, between Brahmin and untouchable, between bourgeoisie and proletariat. But the Bible teaches that the line between good and evil divides each human heart. The evil is within us. "Nothing outside a man can make him 'unclean' by going into him," said Jesus. "Rather, it is what comes out of a man that makes him 'unclean' " (Mark 7:15). We all stand guilty before the Judge of the universe. We are all responsible for the brokenness in our world.

Moreover, we all face the same profound consequences, both personally and cosmically. Many people are put off by the very idea of hell or by preaching about an eternal judgment. But the doctrine of hell is historic Christian orthodoxy. God is a God of love, but he is also a God of justice, and justice requires both heaven (reward for righteousness) and hell (punishment for unrighteousness). This divine judgment may sound harsh and inhumane, but the reality of hell is what makes our choices significant and what grants us full human dignity. For if our actions had no ultimate consequences, they would be meaningless. Furthermore, there would be no final moral accountability and therefore no reason for acting morally, which in turn means there would be no basis for a civilized society.

But, the skeptic asks, what about the person who never hears the gospel? The apostle Paul tells us that all are without excuse because "what may be known about God is plain to them" (Rom. 1:19-20). We are accountable for what we know (and by implication *not* for what we *don't* know). And when we rebel against what we know to be right and true, we eventually pay the consequences.

Even so, God always leaves us a way out. He is ready and willing to forgive and restore us. Full redemption, as we shall see in the next section, is God's provision for sparing us the consequences we rightly deserve.

BONDAGE TO DECAY

The consequences of sin affect the very order of the universe itself. Most people have a narrow understanding of the term *sin*. We tend to think it means that we have broken a few rules, made a few mistakes. So we apologize and get on with our lives, right?

Wrong. Sin is much more than breaking the rules. God created an intricate, interwoven cosmos, each part depending on the others, all governed by laws of order and harmony. Sin affects every part of that order and harmony—twisting, fracturing, distorting, and corrupting it.

First, sin disrupts our relationship with God. What was the first thing Adam and Eve did after they ate the forbidden fruit? They tried to hide from God. Because of sin, humans feel guilty and afraid of God. This is not some neurotic, false guilt, some dysfunctional barrier to living a full, uninhibited life, as modern psychiatry often contends. No, real guilt is an internal signal that we have done something wrong, just as pain is a signal we have done something harmful to our body. When we put a hand on a hot stove, pain tells us that we need to change something we're doing. (We need to take our hand off the burner!) Guilt works the same way. It is an awareness in the core of our being that we have violated the law that governs the universe and have shattered our relationship with the Creator.

Second, sin alienates us from each other. Adam immediately began to blame Eve for his action; Eve, in turn, blamed the serpent for tempting her. ("The devil made me do it.") Evasion, blaming, finger-pointing, superiority, bitterness, and pride— all the elements of social breakdown are right there in the early chapters of Genesis.

Third, the Fall affects all of nature. Because Adam and Eve were given dominion over the rest of creation, their rebellion injected disorder into all of creation. This is a difficult concept to grasp in our scientific age, but Scripture clearly teaches that sin ruptured the physical as well as the moral order. God warned Eve that, as a consequence of sin, childbearing and family life would become a matter of pain and sorrow (see Gen. 3). Certainly it is in our intimate family relationships that we suffer the deepest heartbreak. Then God warned Adam that when he

tried to cultivate the earth to grow food, it would produce
"thorns and thistles" (Gen. 3:17-19). Work, which was originally
creative and fulfilling, would became a matter of drudgery and
toil.

Finally, God told Adam and Eve that they would return to the
dust from which they were taken. In other words, death and its
preliminaries—sickness and suffering—would become part of the
human experience. Death "had no place in the original creation,"
writes C. S. Lewis; it entered our experience because the physical
world itself—including our physical bodies—was damaged by the
Fall. "It is not the soul's nature to leave the body; rather, the body
(denatured by the Fall) deserts the soul."[5] Creation itself is in
"bondage to decay" until the final redemption (Rom. 8:21).

Clearly, the Fall was not just an isolated act of disobedience
that could be quickly mended. Every part of God's good handiwork was marred by the human mutiny. This is why the
Reformers described human nature as "totally depraved." They
did not mean that human nature is completely corrupted, for
in the midst of our sin, we still bear the image of God, just as a
child's sweet face shows through smudges of mud and dirt. Total
depravity, according to the Reformers, means that every part of
our being—intellect, will, emotions, and body—shows the effects
of sin. No part remains untouched by the Fall.

For example, sexuality is good, created by God; but it is often
distorted by lust and unfaithfulness. Similarly, government was
created to maintain order; but it easily degenerates into tyranny
and oppression. The human capacity for artistic creativity is good;
but it can be twisted into messages of rebellion and license. At
the Fall, every part of creation was plunged into the chaos of
sin, and every part cries out for redemption. Only the Christian
worldview keeps these two truths in balance: the radical destruction caused by sin and the hope of restoration to the original
created goodness.

PAYING THE PRICE

Only the Christian concept of sin and moral responsibility gives us a rational way to understand and order our lives. An exchange in one of Nancy's college ethics classes illustrates this well. During a discussion on the nature of moral responsibility, one student asked, "Who are we responsible *to?* After all, the notion of responsibility makes no sense unless we are responsible to someone."

"We're responsible to other people," another student volunteered. "For example, if you run over a child, you're responsible to the child's parents."

"But who says?" persisted the first student. "Who will hold me accountable to those parents?"

"It's society we're responsible to," ventured a third student. "Society sets up the laws that we follow, and it holds us accountable."

"But who gives society that right?" asked the first student.

The answer lurking in many of the students' minds was that our ultimate responsibility is to God. Any other authority can be challenged. Only if there is an absolute Being, a Being of perfect goodness and justice, is there an ultimate tribunal before which we are all accountable. But in a secular university classroom, no one dared say that. So the students debated back and forth, hoping to find some basis for moral accountability that would not require them to acknowledge divine authority.

The university classroom is not the only place where "God talk" is taboo. In many parts of contemporary culture, it is acceptable to believe in God, but only if you keep your belief in a private box. Yet Christianity will not remain privatized. It is not merely a personal belief. It is the truth about all reality. Christians must learn how to break out of the box, to penetrate environments hostile to our faith, make people see the dilemma they themselves face, and then show them why the Christian worldview is the only rational answer.

Nonbelievers must be made to see that they are in an intolerable dilemma. On one hand, we all implicitly hope to live in a society where divine authority is respected, where we don't have to be afraid of being cheated, robbed, or murdered. Yet at the same time, many of us don't want to submit to that divine authority ourselves; we don't want to recognize an external, transcendent source of moral truth that restricts our own behavior. That would be a blow to human pride and self-centeredness, and a denial that choice is our ultimate right, that we are morally autonomous. What's worse, it would mean that when we fail to live up to that transcendent truth, we are in the very uncomfortable position of having not only to admit guilt before the divine tribunal but also to accept the consequences. This is the price we pay for accepting the Christian answer.

And yet the price for rejecting it is much higher. When morality is reduced to personal preferences and when no one can be held morally accountable, society quickly falls into disorder. Entertainers churn out garbage that vulgarizes our children's tastes; politicians tickle our ears while picking our pockets; criminals terrorize our city streets; parents neglect their children; and children grow up without a moral conscience. Then, when social anarchy becomes widespread in any nation, its citizens become prime candidates for a totalitarian-style leader (or leader class) to step in and offer to fix everything. Sadly, by that time many people are so sick of the anarchy and chaos that they readily exchange their freedom for the restoration of social order—even under an iron fist. The Germans did exactly this in the 1930s when they welcomed Hitler; so did the Italians, eagerly following Mussolini, who promised to make the trains run on time.

We must ask people to face the stark choice: either a worldview that maintains that we are inherently good or a worldview that acknowledges a transcendent standard and our accountability before a holy God for our sin. The first choice eventually leads to

t: How can God be good and still allow evil? In
of distress, believers and nonbelievers alike face this
ontradiction. Why would a loving God allow his crea-
ffer? Even the most brilliant mind of our century was
this question, and in his case it formed a tragic barrier
im and the God that he knew must exist.

moral anarchy and opens the door to tyranny; the second choice makes possible an ordered and morally responsible society. When Jewish theologian Dennis Prager gives speeches, he often asks audiences to imagine that they are walking down a dark city alley at night and they suddenly see a group of young men coming toward them. Prager then asks: "Would you be frightened or relieved that they are carrying Bibles and that they've just come from a Bible study?" Audiences invariably laugh and admit that they would be relieved.[6] Commitment to biblical truth leads to more civil behavior.

By contrast, no one looking at the history of our own century should be able to swallow the notion that if only we liberate people from oppressive moral traditions and rules, they will be spontaneously good and generous. Every civilization from the beginning of time has known that lawlessness leads to cruelty and barbarism. Even thieves have codes of honor, as the saying goes. Moral laws are not stifling rules that repress and restrict our true nature; rather, they are directions for becoming the kind of beings God intended when he created us. When we understand this, we see that moral standards are life-giving, life-enhancing, life-enriching truths.

The case needs to be made that a realistic, biblical doctrine of sin is the only safeguard against both the personal tyranny of a Charles Dederich and the impersonal tyranny of an overbearing state. It was acceptance of the biblical doctrine of sin that gave Americans the historically unprecedented degree of freedom that we still enjoy today. Our founders built checks and balances on all branches of government because they recognized the need to contain ambition and greed. As James Madison put it, these structures "pit ambition against ambition and make it impossible for any element of government to obtain unchecked power."[7] Such limits on power protect us much better than any written document guaranteeing human rights. After all, the constitution of the former Soviet Union contained a list of rights even more extensive than our own Bill of Rights, but the document didn't do any good without limits on power.

We need to press our skeptical neighbors to spin out the logical consequences of their worldviews. Denying the reality of sin may appear to be enlightened and uplifting, but ultimately it is demeaning and destructive. It denies the significance of our choices and actions, and it unleashes our worst impulses. Christianity, on the other hand, enables us to address societal issues such as welfare, crime, human rights, and education. Christianity provides the basis for a welfare system that is both compassionate and morally challenging, reinforcing recipients' dignity and self-respect. Christianity undergirds a criminal justice system that holds people accountable for their actions rather than reduces their stature as moral agents through the psychobabble of victimization. Christianity affords the basis for a solid theory of human rights, regarding all individuals as equally created by God and equally fallen. Christian education treats children with the dignity of beings made in the image of God. In each of these areas, as we have seen in the preceding chapters, a comparison exposes the utter bankruptcy of modern utopianism and its central tenet of natural goodness.

TURNING THE TABLES

Of course, the notion of sin is not just a worldview issue; it is also intensely personal. On that level, a realistic grasp of human depravity drives us to God in our search for a solution to our personal guilt. Instead of trying to bury it under layers of psychological jargon—where it never stays buried—we can face our guilt head-on, knowing that God himself has provided a way out.

We frequently hear it said that religion is merely wish fulfillment. This was Freud's argument: Christianity is an illusion we

invent to meet various personal nee
psychological benefits to be derived
psychological reductionism is a gam
can be said that there are likewise co
from *not* believing in God. After all
disconcerting as it is comforting (at
wants to abandon personal preferen
to an absolute moral standard for ev
wants to go beyond admitting to a f
fess to having sinned before a holy (
one's wealth? Who wants to suffer f

Indeed, we could argue that the n
which modern culture has succumbe
psychology of atheism, which is itse
a deep desire to be free from all exte
transcendent source of morality. It c
believe the dogma of the autonomo
there are no objective truths making
that right and wrong are subject to c
own decisions we create values out o
a mini-god, creating his or her own
consign their own children to death
did.

No God, no sin, no guilt. Human
well with the world. No wonder the
tially, to be so attractive.

By turning the tables in this way,
strategy of relegating ideas to the gar
cuts both ways. And then we can ste
the real issue: the straightforward cla
It matches our own experience better
It fits reality. It makes sense. It answ

And yet, there is one question tha

some poi
moments
seeming
tures to s
stymied l
between

A God who did not abolish suffering—worse, a God who abolished sin precisely by suffering—is a scandal to the modern mind. PETER KREEFT

CHAPTER 7

DOES SUFFERING MAKE SENSE?

As you read, keep the following questions in mind:
- What did Einstein believe (and not believe) that kept him from accepting the God of the Bible?
- What five false solutions are commonly given to solve "the problem of evil"?
- Why is it important that we recognize the nature of freedom and the historicity of the "Fall"?
- What role does justice play in the grand story of God and mankind?

The year was 1942, and the scene was the crowded front parlor of Albert Einstein's home, where the famous physicist had arranged a tea party for three clergymen: a young orthodox rabbi named Dov Hertzen, a middle-aged Catholic priest named Brian McNaughton, and a liberal Protestant theologian named Mark Hartman.[1]

"Rabbi Hertzen here 'provoked' this little party," Einstein began, as soon as the men had sampled the tea and cookies. "He congratulated me on my open-mindedness when I dropped my belief in a static universe. Not long ago, I observed Hubble's red shifts for myself at Cal Tech."

Einstein leaned back in his chair and lifted his chin. "Of course, I have known for a long time that one of the implications of general relativity is that the universe is expanding. And if it is expanding, then clearly in the past it was once smaller. Extrapolate backward in time, and you end up with a universe that began at some finite time in the past as a superdense ball.

"And so," Einstein concluded, folding his hands, "I have come to accept that the universe had a real beginning in time. But what are the consequences of this discovery? Does it have any metaphysical, or even religious, implications? This is what Rabbi Hertzen asked me, and I thought perhaps we could discuss it together."

He smiled briefly. With his tousled hair and bushy mustache, his old sweater and slacks, Einstein was a master at creating the stereotype of the gentle, absentminded professor. But he used his famous image ruthlessly, disarming people, then wielding his sharp logic to cut them to shreds.

Rabbi Hertzen fell for the ruse immediately. Perched on the edge of his chair, he plunged in eagerly. "Don't you think, if the universe itself had a beginning, there must be a cause behind it? A capital *C* Cause?"

"And why is this conclusion necessary?" Einstein gave the young rabbi a sharp look over his teacup, then added in a friendlier tone, "I know something of science, but when we begin to speak of a capital *C,* we have passed beyond the bounds of science."

"This much, at least, remains scientific," Father McNaughton broke in, calmly gesturing with the cigarette wedged between his fingers. "If we observe an effect, we infer a cause. If the universe had a beginning in time, that event must have a cause—a cause *outside* the universe."

"Bravo," Einstein said archly. "You have just reduced the question to a simple syllogism."

"Sometimes the truth is simple," McNaughton retorted with a smile. The group laughed nervously.

Rabbi Hertzen resumed his argument, his voice slightly shrill with agitation. "The findings of astronomers are giving scientific confirmation that there must be an almighty Being. As a Jew, Dr. Einstein, don't you have every reason to find out whether or not this Being is the One who gave Moses the Torah? The almighty One, blessed be He, of the Jewish people. Your own people," he finished triumphantly.

"How could any almighty being *not* be the God of the Jewish people?" Einstein asked dryly.

"So you do believe in a creator?" the rabbi pressed.

"I have said it before and I will say it again: I believe in Spinoza's God, a deity revealed in the orderly harmony of the universe."[2] He leaned forward for emphasis, warming to his subject. "As a scientist, whenever I find a way to reduce disparate events to some underlying unity of natural law, I am moved by reverence for the rationality at the heart of reality. For me, this attitude seems to be religious in the highest sense of the word. I call it cosmic religious feeling."[3]

The faces of his three guests brightened, while Einstein drew on his pipe, permitting them this momentary hope. "But what I *cannot* accept," he went on, "is the idea of a personal God who punishes or rewards people. My religion has no dogma, no personal God created in man's image. A real scientist must be convinced of the universal operation of the law of causation, and he cannot for a moment entertain the idea of a being who interferes in the course of events."

Einstein's voice grew louder. "Why do you religious leaders attach your conception of God to the myths of the past? I tell you, you do religion a disservice by keeping up this primitive notion. It's the major cause of conflict between science and religion."

He jabbed his pipe and glared from one man to another. "I know what it is. Your religion has been a tool for control. You use it to fill people with fear and concentrate power in the hands of priests. That's why you cling to it—to increase your own power."[4]

Taken aback, his three guests scrambled mentally for a response. Einstein took advantage of their silence.

"Forgive me for my vehemence. You are, after all, my guests. But please, consider—the argument is really simple. If this personal being is omnipotent, then every event everywhere in the universe is his work—including every human action, every human thought, every human feeling. So how is it possible to think of holding people responsible for their deeds and thoughts before such an almighty being?"

His voice dropped to a steely intensity. "You say God is a being of absolute goodness and righteousness. But think of this. If he is the one ultimately responsible for our actions, then he is behind all the harm we do each other. In giving out punishments and rewards, he is in a way passing judgment on himself. God himself is the source of the very evil he supposedly judges!"[5]

Father McNaughton was the first to recover. "But we have free will," he began.

"This I do not believe," Einstein interrupted. "Science reveals a universe utterly bound by natural laws, a rational universe. There is simply no room left for causes of a different nature."

"If we have no free will, how can there be morality?" asked Rabbi Hertzen.

"Free will. Free will. Don't you see, it's an illusion?" Einstein rubbed his forehead and closed his eyes briefly, beginning to weary of this fruitless exchange. "When science has probed the depths of the human mind, I am convinced we will find the laws that govern it, just like everything else. So, please, don't rest your arguments for God on arguments for free will. Your religion is constantly being forced to retreat before the advances of science."[6]

As Einstein picked up his teacup, Reverend Hartman finally found his opening. "Really," he said soothingly, "we don't have to argue science versus religion. Religion doesn't make any claims about the world known by science. Genuine religion is a feeling of dependence on the Absolute."

"Hmmm," Einstein said, crumbling a cookie. "I know you to be a progressive, forward-thinking man, Reverend. So how do you explain away the problem of a God who causes evil?" His eyes glinted.

"Oh, I have no quarrel with science or its teaching that we are part of a universe governed by natural laws. But religion belongs in the realm of human experience. We give meaning to suffering by believing in a God of love and redemption."

"I see," said Einstein evenly. "We know religion is false, but we believe anyway to meet our psychological needs."

"No!" exclaimed Rabbi Hertzen. "God allows suffering because we learn by it."

Einstein took a deep breath and raised his eyebrows cryptically. "Yes, I'm afraid we do," he said. "This has been a most interesting afternoon, gentlemen. But I have a headache and should rest before dinner."

After his guests had left, Einstein wandered over to his music stand and began shuffling idly through the sheet music. His eye caught the title of a piece he had played recently on his violin: Bach's "Jesu, Joy of Man's Desiring."

With a snort Einstein gave vent to the impatience and frustration that had been building all afternoon. He knew well what had motivated his little tea party. He had long nursed a smoldering anger about the suffering of the Jewish race through the centuries, and now ominous rumors were coming out of Germany. No, he could not accept the idea of a personal God who allowed such things to happen. And this afternoon's conversation had brought him no closer to an answer.

Better to escape into the world of science, where order and rationality offered an alternative to the chaotic pain of personal life. He opened his violin case and fingered the strings of his instrument. For that matter, music was almost as good an escape. In music he found the symmetry, the fundamental simplicity, the rational perfection that he craved—the same order he found in his scientific work.[7]

He took out his violin and started tuning up. Music would take his mind off these troubling questions that had no answers.

EINSTEIN'S DILEMMA

For Albert Einstein, the greatest scientist of this century, the toughest intellectual barrier to Christian faith was not the question of whether God created the world. He saw clearly that the universe is designed and orderly, and he concluded that it must, therefore, be the result of a mind, not merely of matter bumping around endlessly in space. As he put it, the order of the universe "reveals an intelligence of such superiority" that it overshadows all human intelligence.[8] His famous quip, "God does not play dice with the universe," though directed specifically against quantum theory, reveals his fierce commitment to a causal order unifying nature from top to bottom.

No, what stymied Einstein was something much tougher than the doctrine of creation: It was the problem of evil and suffering. Knowing there must be a designer, he agonized over the *character* of that designer. How could God be good yet allow terrible things to happen to people? And because Einstein could not reconcile the problem of evil and suffering with a good God, he turned away from the God of the Bible.

What tripped Einstein up was that he was a determinist. He viewed human beings as complicated machines, doing what they are programmed to do by natural forces, like windup toys. But if that is so, then there can be no such thing as morality, sin, or guilt. If a person's actions are determined, Einstein wrote, then "in God's eyes he cannot be responsible" for his behavior, any more than a stone is responsible for where it flies when someone throws it.[9]

Who *is* responsible then? God himself, Einstein had to conclude. If an omnipotent God exists, he reasoned, there must be a kind of divine determinism, where God winds us up and makes us act the way we do. But if God makes us do bad things as well as good, then he is directly responsible for evil. "In giving out punishments and rewards, he would to a certain extent be passing judgment on himself," Einstein wrote. "How can this be combined with the goodness and righteousness ascribed to him?"[10] If our actions are determined, then God himself must be evil.

Unwilling to accept the hopelessness of a belief system in which the ultimate reality is evil, Einstein concluded that the only God that exists is an impersonal cosmic mind giving the world its rational structure. In saying he believed in Spinoza's God, Einstein meant he believed in the principle of order in the universe. To Einstein, true religion was nothing more than rapture before the rational structure of the universe.[11]

Einstein was nothing if not logical. But a person's conclusion is only as good as his premise, and Einstein's premise—that humans are essentially robots—was seriously flawed. He missed the truth of Judaism (into which he was born) and of Christianity (which he also investigated) not because he was forced to by "the facts," but because he had already committed himself to a particular philosophy—a philosophy that prevented him from reconciling the existence of suffering and evil with the existence of a good God.

Many people share Einstein's predicament, finding the problem of evil a major stumbling block to Christian faith. So how can we respond? Does the Bible offer a sound answer that makes sense of suffering? Can Christianity answer the heart's demand for justice in a fallen universe?

THE PROBLEM OF EVIL

To see the problem clearly, let's state it in simple propositions.
If God is both all-good and all-powerful, he will not allow evil
and suffering to exist in his creation. Yet evil does exist. Therefore, either God is not all-good (that's why he tolerates evil), or he
is not all-powerful (that's why he can't get rid of evil, even though
he wants to). Throughout history, people have grappled with this
apparent contradiction and have proposed a variety of solutions,
all of which fall short of the biblical solution. Since we encounter
these solutions again and again, it is important to know why they
are inadequate and false. Let's examine five of the most common
false solutions.

Solution #1: Deny that God exists at all. The atheist simply
throws out the first proposition. If there is no God, then evil
poses no problem. Or does it?

If we follow this proposal to its logical conclusion, the problem
of evil is transformed into something even worse: that *nothing* is
evil, and, by extension, that nothing is good. For if there is no
God, then "good" and "evil" are nothing more than subjective
feelings that reflect what our culture has taught us to approve
or disapprove, or what we individually happen to like or dislike.
For the atheist there is no answer to the question of evil because
there is really no question. There *is* no such thing as objective
evil; we are merely projecting our subjective feelings onto external
events.

But does this satisfy the innate human outrage over evil and
suffering? Of course not. Instead, it mocks us by reducing our
deepest moral convictions to a trick of our minds. We may be
robbed, our children may be murdered, we may die a lingering
death, but none of this is genuinely evil. It is merely part of nature
because nature is all that exists. We may cry out in the night
for answers, but objective reality is indifferent to our tears. Poet
Stephen Crane portrays this dilemma poignantly:

A man said to the universe,
"Sir, I exist."
"However," replied the universe,
"The fact has not created in me
A sense of obligation."[12]

On its own terms, atheism simply has no answer, and the point-lessness of our suffering makes it all the more painful.

Ironically, though, when things go horribly wrong, even die-hard atheists shake their fists at heaven; even those who say God does not exist instinctively blame him for their sorrows. There are no atheists in foxholes, as the saying goes. So let's move on to various religious answers.

Solution #2: Deny that suffering exists. Some people attempt to solve the problem by casting evil and suffering as illusions created by our own minds. This is the strategy adopted by Christian Science and by some Eastern religions. The physical universe is an illusion (*maya* in Hinduism), and the suffering of the body is a misconception of the mind. If we train ourselves to think cor-rectly, we can overcome suffering through realizing that it does not exist.

But can anyone really live consistently with such a philosophy of denial? The story is told of a boy who went to a Christian Science practitioner and asked him to pray for his father, who was very ill. "Your father only *thinks* he is sick," the man told the boy. "He must learn to counter those negative thoughts and realize he is actually healthy." The next day the boy came back, and the min-ister asked how his father was doing. "Today he thinks he's dead," replied the boy. The power of positive thinking cannot erase the objective reality of suffering and death.

During my White House days, I personally witnessed the futility of trying to pretend evil is not real. Among President Nixon's small circle of top advisors were four Christian Scientists, including Bob

Haldeman and the late John Ehrlichman, the two men closest to the president during the critical months following the Watergate break-in, when the cover-up was being fashioned. One evening during the scandal, I met with Bob Haldeman and warned him that any cover-up would imperil the presidency. The tough-minded chief of staff swung around in his chair and glared at me.

"What would you do?" he demanded.

"Don't provide any money to the burglars who broke into the Watergate offices," I suggested. "It could be considered hush money."

Haldeman brushed aside my caution with a steely gaze. "Everyone has defense funds," he said.

I kept pressing. "Bob, the president needs a good criminal defense attorney to advise him."

"Nah," Haldeman replied. "We've done nothing wrong. What he needs is just a good PR man."

With Nixon's chief advisors assuring him that his only problem was public image, he was never forced to confront reality. Like King David, he needed a Nathan to be brutally honest with him. (How I wish I had done that.)

But could it have been their worldview that caused Haldeman and Ehrlichman to keep reducing wrongdoing to a problem of perception? In the words of Glenn Tinder, "A logical Christian Scientist does not deplore and try to eradicate sinful desires but tries simply not to notice them. Nor does a logical Christian Scientist who has committed a grave wrong suffer pangs of guilt and seek redemption; rather the whole matter is as far as possible erased from one's mind."[13] Or, perhaps, from the country's mind. Just hire that good PR man.

But the lessons of history tell us that if we do not believe in evil, we cannot cope with the reality when it hits us squarely in the face. The illusion theory simply cannot hold up under the weight of human experience.

Solution #3: Place God beyond good and evil. Some people hold the notion of a God so distant and transcendent that he cannot be defined by any concept in the human mind—a "God who is beyond good and evil." This may sound lofty and reverent, but if the terms *good* and *evil* do not apply to ultimate reality, then they are mere quirks of our own subjective consciousness. The idea of God as "wholly other" makes him so utterly transcendent that our moral outrage finds no echoing outrage in him. We are still left alone with our tears in the night.[14]

Solution #4: God's power is limited. The reasoning here is that an all-powerful God would not allow bad things to happen; since bad things do happen, God must not be all-powerful. This perspective is gaining popularity today through a school of thought known as *process theology,* which proposes a God who is still in the process of becoming—a God who is evolving with the world and is not yet omnipotent. This God has the best of intentions (he really would like to change things), but being finite, he is not able to get rid of the evil that plagues creation. We must direct our hope to the future, when God and the world will reach a glorious new stage of evolution and all ills will be overcome.

This is the theology promoted in Rabbi Kushner's best-seller *When Bad Things Happen to Good People,* which defends God's goodness by denying his omnipotence. "God wants the righteous to live peaceful, happy lives, but sometimes even He can't bring that about," Kushner writes. "It's too difficult even for God to keep cruelty and chaos from claiming their innocent victims."[15] This is a deity who struggles against the forces of chaos, winning some battles and losing others.

Now, such a theology might solve the problem of suffering for future generations, born after God has finally gotten his act together, but it certainly won't solve the problem of suffering and evil for us here and now. This deity is a kind but incompetent heavenly bumbler who has little to offer to the many generations who must suffer and die *before* heaven has evolved here on earth.

Solution #5: God has created evil to achieve a greater good. This is the position taken by philosopher John Hick in *Evil and the God of Love.* Only in a world where we have to struggle for the good can we freely choose God, Hick argues. The struggle itself is necessary to mature the soul and make us ready to enjoy God forever.[16]

This position contains a kernel of truth, for good does sometimes emerge from bad things, and struggle can, indeed, mature the soul. The problem is that if we propose that God created evil *for any reason,* even a good reason, then we are back to Einstein's dilemma: that God himself is evil and there is no escape, no salvation. For if evil is an intrinsic part of reality, it cannot ultimately be eliminated. Besides, <u>if God created human beings in such a way that they require evil in order to mature, then he made them flawed rather than "very good," as Genesis 1 proclaims.</u>

The poet and playwright Archibald MacLeish makes this point in his play *J. B.,* which retells the story of Job in a modern setting. A clergyman tells J. B. that his suffering is caused by the simple fact that he is a human being, for humans are intrinsically flawed. "Your sin is simple. You were born a man."

J. B. finds this explanation singularly uncomforting. "Yours is the cruelest comfort of them all," he responds, "making the Creator of the Universe the miscreator of mankind, a party to the crimes He punishes."[17]

Like Einstein, MacLeish realized that if we say that God created humanity sinful, the implication is that when he judges sin, he judges himself.

Moreover, the notion that God created evil to achieve a greater good is an obvious fallacy, for it is clear that many evil things do not lead to good results. The most gripping expression of this objection comes from the pen of the great Russian novelist Fyodor Dostoyevsky in *The Brothers Karamazov.*

In a challenge to his younger brother, who is a Christian, Ivan Karamazov tells the story of a little girl tormented by her parents. "This poor child of five was subjected to every possible torture by those cultivated parents. They beat her, thrashed her, kicked her for no reason till her body was one bruise." Then Ivan turns on his brother, demanding an answer. "Can you understand why a little creature who can't even understand what's done to her should beat her little aching heart with her tiny fist in the dark and weep her meek, unresentful tears to dear, kind God to protect her? Do you understand . . . why this infamy must be and is permitted?"[18]

For himself, Ivan insists, he will not accept a God who allows the pointless suffering of even one tiny child. "Imagine that you are creating a fabric of human destiny with the object of making men happy in the end, giving them peace and rest at last, but that it was essential and inevitable to torture to death only one tiny creature—that baby beating its breast with its fist, for instance— and to found that edifice on its avenged tears, would you worship the architect on those conditions?"[19]

The answer must be no. No sensitive person could respond otherwise. But the problem lies in the premise: the assumption that God requires evil, even as a temporary stage, to complete creation's destiny. The God of Scripture does not need to build a temporary hell in order to produce heaven. Of course, once evil exists, God can and often does wring good from it. But that is a very different point (as we will see later).

So why is there evil in the world? How do we find any meaning in our suffering? None of the alternatives described above satisfies the cry of the human heart. Every one of them either diminishes God or diminishes us. Only the biblical explanation is consistent with both reason and human experience, for it alone tells us how God can be God—the ultimate reality and Creator of all things— and yet not be responsible for evil.

FREEDOM TO CHOOSE

How does the Bible reconcile God's goodness and power with
the presence of evil? Scripture teaches that God is good and
that he created a universe that was "very good." It also teaches
that the universe is now marred by evil, death, and suffering.
Logically there is only one way to reconcile these two state-
ments *without* denying any element in them: *There must be a
source of sin outside of God.* And that is exactly what Scripture
tells us.

God is good and created a perfect world. But one of the
things that makes humans (and angels) intelligent beings is freedom. They had the freedom to obey God or to turn away from
him. And to turn away from God, the source of all goodness, is
to create evil. Evil does not have an independent existence, nor
was it created by God. Evil is created by sin.

The decision to sin was made in the spiritual realm by Satan
and other angels, who are intelligent beings capable of genuine
moral choice; sin then entered our world through the free moral
choices made by the first human beings, Adam and Eve. From
there, the plague has spread through all of history because of the
free moral choices humans continue to make.

People sometimes ask, What made Adam and Eve sin? But
freedom means there *is* no external cause. We are not trapped in
an endless chain of cause and effect, as determinists like Einstein
believe. Instead, we can initiate a genuinely new chain of cause
and effect. In making moral choices, we are genuine first causes;
and logically you can't ask what caused a first cause. Thus we
can resolve the apparent contradiction we began with: God is
all-good, and he created a world that was good and perfect; but
one of the perfect things he made was free creatures, and they
have freely chosen to do wrong.

As we said earlier, it is vital that we recognize the historicity
of the Fall. If the Fall is merely a symbol, while in reality sin is

intrinsic to human nature, then we are back to Einstein's dilemma: that God created evil and is implicated in our wrongdoing. Scripture gives a genuine answer to the problem of evil only because it insists that God created the world originally good—and that sin entered at a particular point in history. And when that happened, it caused a cataclysmic change, distorting and disfiguring creation, resulting in death and destruction. That's why evil is so hateful, so repulsive, so tragic. Our response is entirely appropriate, and the only reason God can truly comfort us is that *he's on our side*. He did not create evil, and he, too, hates the way it has disfigured his handiwork.

WHY DID GOD CREATE US CAPABLE OF SINNING?

But if God knew beforehand that we would make such a mess of things, says the skeptic, why did he let it happen? Why did he create us capable of sinning? Fair question. But think carefully about what it means. In order for God to ensure that we *could not* sin, he would have had to tamper with our freedom of will—to create us not as full human beings but as puppets or robots programmed to do only what he wanted. But that would have rendered us incapable of loving God or one another, for genuine love cannot be coerced.[20] Also, without free will, we would not be capable of moral responsibility, creativity, obedience, loyalty, or heroism. The only way God could create beings that are fully human was to take the risk that they would use their freedom to choose evil.

Then, once humans did choose evil, God's holy character required justice. He could not ignore it, overlook it, or simply wipe the slate clean and start over again. Once the scales of justice had been tipped, they had to be balanced. Once the moral fabric of the universe had been torn, it had to be mended.

JUSTICE, MERCY, AND LOVE

In that case, says the skeptic, the human race should have ended
with Adam and Eve. They should have been punished for their
rebellion, cast into hell, and that would have been the end of
human history. Ah, but God is merciful as well as just, and he
devised an astonishing alternative: He himself would bear the
punishment for his creatures. God himself would enter the world
of humanity to suffer the judgment and death that sinful humans
deserved. And that is exactly what he did, through the God-man,
Jesus Christ.

This was not what anyone ever would have expected; it was not
anything humans could have devised. Jesus met the demands of
divine justice by accepting execution on a Roman cross. He beat
Satan at his own game: He took the worst that Satan and human
sin could mete out, and he turned it into the means of our salvation. "By his wounds we are healed," writes Isaiah (Isa. 53:5).
Through his death on the cross, Jesus defeated evil and guaranteed
the ultimate victory over it. At the end of time there will be a new
heaven and a new earth, free of sin and suffering, where he will
"wipe every tear from their eyes" (Rev. 21:4).

Until that time, God uses the "thorns and thistles" that have
infested creation since the Fall to teach, chastise, sanctify, and
transform us, making us ready for that new heaven and earth.
This is something I well understand: The greatest blessings in my
life have emerged from suffering, and I have seen the same process
repeated in countless lives. Just as it hurts when the doctor sets a
broken bone, so it can cause enormous pain when God resets our
character. Yet it is the only way to be whole and healthy.

An ancient document describing the martyrs of the church in
the first century says that they "attained such towering strength
of soul that not one of them uttered a cry or groan."[21] Through
suffering, God gives all who turn to him "towering strength of
soul." Because we are fallen creatures, it often takes suffering to

detach us from our wrong habits, our mistaken notions, and the idols we live for, so that our hearts are free to love God.

Friedrich Nietzsche, though himself an atheist, once uttered a profoundly biblical truth: "Men and women can endure any amount of suffering so long as they know the why to their existence."[22] The Bible gives us "the why," the wider context of meaning and purpose, an eternal perspective. God's purposes are the context that give suffering meaning and significance.

In his famous doctrine of "Blessed Fault," Augustine encapsulated the mystery of suffering: "God judged it better to bring good out of evil than to suffer no evil at all."[23] Better to endure the pain involved in redeeming sinners than not to create human beings at all.

Why did he do that? There is only one answer. Love. God loved us so much that even when he foresaw the sin and suffering that would darken and distort his creation, he chose to create us anyway. That is the most profound mystery of all, and one that inspires our hearts to worship.

DISCUSSION QUESTIONS

CHAPTER 6

1 Review the extended (two-paragraph) definition of *obedience* at the beginning of the chapter. Does this definition ring true in your experience of a healthy, obedient child-parent relationship? If not, how would you change the definition?

2 We have a choice whether or not to obey a transcendent standard of right and wrong. How does this statement differ from the meaning and context of the word *choice* as used by secularists who advocate for a self-defined "good"? Discuss this in relation to "the Great Lie" at the heart of Satan's temptation of Eve.

3 What is so important about the grounded "goodness" of God's creation, as repeatedly reported in Genesis 1?

4 Read aloud Isaiah 14:12-15. Although the king of Babylon is the immediate object of this poetic prophecy, the story of Satan's condemnation lies in the background. What attitude

in Satan brought his downfall? How does this attitude creep into the Garden of Eden?

5 Read aloud Revelation 12:9-10, 17. What additional insights are given into Satan and his "mission"? (See also Scripture passages cited in the chapter 6 text.)

6 What is significant about the fact that Adam and Eve's sin is not simply a mythical fable?

7 Following the "Sin Affects All" heading in the text, what "all" aspects are significant to a biblical view of sin and why?

8 What "intolerable dilemma" do nonbelievers face? How can this lead to "the personal tyranny of a Charles Dederich and the impersonal tyranny of an overbearing state"? What makes the Christian view of sin a tolerable alternative?

9 Freud argued that Christianity was an illusionary way of fulfilling a wish. Conversely, give reasons why being an atheist might be an illusionary way of fulfilling a wish.

CHAPTER 7

10 What did Einstein believe (and not believe) that kept him from accepting the God of the Bible?

11 Summarize in a clear, concise way the flaw in each of the five false solutions to the problem of evil. (How does each diminish God or us as humans?)

12 If someone asked you, "What made Adam and Eve sin?" what answer would you give?

13 If we did not have free will, what would humanity be like?

14 What hope do you see in the material covered in this session?

ROLE PLAY
Refer to the directions for role play at the end of session 1 (pp. 40–41).

CONVERSATION STARTERS
    a. Assume you're having coffee with a neighbor who, like Einstein, says he just cannot believe in a good God who

would allow such suffering in the world. Ask some leading questions that help you understand which false solution to the problem of evil and suffering the person holds. In conversation present a biblical alternative.

 b. Assume someone says, "If God is both all-loving and all-powerful, why doesn't he use his power to stop suffering and injustice?"

CLOSING SUMMARY

What is the one thing you want to remember from what you read (or heard or did) in this session?

Consider sharing this with the group.

REDEEMED:
HOW THEY LOVE
TO PROCLAIM IT

GOOD INTENTIONS

As you read this chapter, which is the first in a group of chapters that address the third worldview question— What can we do to fix it?—keep the following questions in mind:

- What factors led to Dr. Nathanson's change of heart regarding abortion?
- What do you learn about Dr. Nathanson's spiritual journey and spiritual need?

The bank of operating-room lamps cast a glaring light over the patient as Dr. Bernard Nathanson surveyed the scene with a practiced clinical eye from beneath his bushy black eyebrows. Heavy white sheets covered the woman's upper body; her knees were bent, her feet in the stirrups. Forty minutes ago she had been prepped with a tranquilizer to ease her anxiety.

Nathanson positioned the speculum to hold open the vaginal canal, then administered a local anesthetic to the cervix with a hypodermic. He widened the cervical canal with a metal rod and inserted the curette (a long metal instrument with a sharp-edged steel loop at the end) into the uterine cavity. The patient was about nine weeks pregnant—far enough along that it took Nathanson an extra minute or two to be sure that all of the inner layer of the uterus was scraped away and the tissue collected for examination.

At the end of the ten-minute procedure, Nathanson carefully

examined the lumps of bloody tissue on the tray to make sure
that he could account for all the parts of the dismembered fetus.
Having satisfied himself that the procedure was successfully completed, Nathanson turned away from the gurney, nodded to the
nurse, and stripped off his surgical gloves. After dropping them in
the disposal bin, he brushed his hands in a dismissive but satisfied
gesture. He'd done a good job. Quite routine, yet one did want to
maintain high standards.

He stepped over and looked down into the face of the woman
under the white sheet.

"Everything's fine," he said. "Rest for a while in the recovery
room; then I'll come check on you. You have someone to take you
home, right?"

The woman nodded, licking her dry lips.

Nathanson headed for the swinging doors leading to the sur-
geon's rest area, where he would take a short break before return-
ing to the table for the afternoon patients. Another lineup of
terrified, often grief-stricken women.

No one watching the scene in the operating room would have
guessed that the woman on the gurney was Nathanson's lover . . .
or that he had just aborted his own child.[1]

SNAPPED INTO FOCUS

For Dr. Bernard Nathanson in the mid-1960s this scene typified
the new world of reproductive freedom. He had campaigned
vigorously for the legalization of abortion, and in his eyes, his
intentions were good and reasonable. Even righteous. After all,
when he had begun his residency at the obstetric and gynecologic
clinic at New York's Woman's Hospital ten years earlier, he had
seen hundreds of emergency cases resulting from illegal abortions.
And the outcomes differed markedly, depending on the woman's
social and economic situation.

Poor women arrived hemorrhaging badly, running high fevers, in shock. They had either attempted to induce abortion themselves, using crude instruments, or they had been butchered by quacks. The massive infections that often followed frequently resulted in sterility, and many times they led to the need for a hysterectomy. Some women even died.

By contrast, affluent private patients had it easy. Together with sympathetic doctors, they contrived ways of faking miscarriages, which meant that Nathanson and other residents would then perform a D & C (dilation and curettage, a procedure that scrapes the uterine wall). Or the women simply flew off to Puerto Rico, England, or Japan and had the procedure done there.

It was this social inequity that first motivated Bernard Nathanson to campaign for the legalization of abortion. In 1969, he teamed up with Lawrence Lader to found the National Abortion Rights Action League (then known as the National Association for the Repeal of Abortion Laws). The organization helped to enlist feminists, including Betty Friedan, in the cause of abortion on demand; but it was the two men, Nathanson and Lader, who crafted the movement's strategy against its most formidable opponents and did much to define abortion as a "woman's issue" on which only feminists are permitted to express an opinion. It was also Nathanson and Lader who determined that the Catholic hierarchy should be demonized as an elite club of white males who were insensitive to women's problems.

In 1970, when New York liberalized its abortion laws, Nathanson began running the nation's largest abortion clinic, the Center for Reproductive and Sexual Health (known to staff members by its acronym, CRASH). Located in Manhattan, the facility thrived on referrals from the Reverend Howard Moody's Clergy Consultation Service on Abortion, a network of Protestant ministers and Jewish rabbis. Nathanson took pride in the clinic's high professional standards and in the success of its outpatient surgical model.

In 1973, however, when *Roe v. Wade* made abortion on demand legal across the country, Nathanson decided to make a career change. He accepted a position as chief of obstetrical service at St. Luke's Hospital Center and went from tending mothers to tending babies (although he continued to perform abortions). His task was to organize a sophisticated perinatology unit, complete with electronic fetal-monitoring machines and other expensive equipment to treat ailing newborns.

At the time, one of the most exciting new gadgets was the ultrasound machine, which literally opened a window on fetal development. The first time Nathanson saw an ultrasound in action, he was with a group of residents gathered around a pregnant patient in a darkened examining room, watching a demonstration by a technician.[2]

The technician applied a conductive gel to the woman's abdomen and then began working a handheld sensor over her stomach. As the splatter on the video screen clarified, Nathanson was amazed. He could see a throbbing heart! When the technician focused closely on the image, Nathanson could see all four chambers pumping. It looked like an animated blossom, with such thickness and definition that it took his breath away. He could also see the major vessels leading to and from the cardiac rose.

The technician next brought the baby's forehead, eyes, and mouth into focus. Then, by zooming out, the technician showed that the baby had its hands folded over its face. Right hand, left hand. On each one, Nathanson counted four fingers and a thumb.

The view from above the crown of the baby's head showed the development of the brain, where the first folds could be seen. Then the technician scanned the elegant architecture of the spine.

Was it a boy or a girl? Just like expectant parents, the group couldn't help wondering. It was a girl. Then finally, the technician showed the bone structure of the legs, and each foot with five perfect toes.

During the course of the scan, Nathanson noticed that his mind had dropped the word *fetus* in favor of *baby*. Suddenly, everything he had been learning about the child in the womb since his entry into the field of perinatology snapped into focus. For example, he knew that a fertilized human egg becomes a self-directed entity very early, after it has multiplied into only four cells; that the heartbeat begins as early as the eighteenth day after conception; that at six weeks the major organ systems have formed. In fact, after only twelve weeks, *no* new anatomical developments occur; the child simply grows larger and more capable of sustaining life outside the womb.

All these had been only medical facts, but now they coalesced with the grainy image on the screen and crashed into Nathanson's consciousness. He felt a chill along his spine, and the air in the room seemed to grow denser, making it hard for him to breathe. His mood swung from the exaltation of new knowledge to a brow-sweating panic as the question hit him: How many babies just like this little girl had he himself cut to pieces? How many human lives had he taken?

"WE ARE TAKING LIFE"

Bernard Nathanson soon became convinced that human life existed within the womb from the onset of pregnancy. In an article he wrote for the *New England Journal of Medicine*, he confessed that at CRASH he had presided over "60,000 deaths." In abortion "we are taking life," he wrote, "and the deliberate taking of life, even of a special order and under special circumstances, is an inexpressibly serious matter." While he did not conclude that abortion was wrong, he did say that physicians "must work together to create a moral climate rich enough to provide for abortion, but sensitive enough to life to accommodate a profound sense of loss."[3]

Nathanson's article caused heated controversy, and the public attention forced him to think even more closely about the morality of abortion.

The article also generated a new development that took Nathanson by surprise. He began receiving invitations to speak at pro-life gatherings—groups that consisted largely of devoutly religious people, whether Catholics, conservative Protestants, or Orthodox Jews. Although Nathanson accepted the invitations, he always made it clear that his objections to abortion were not based on any religious beliefs but proceeded from scientific facts and purely humanitarian conclusions. When his first book, *Aborting America,* was published in 1979, he even criticized what he saw as specious arguments and false rhetoric used by some pro-life activists.

Yet by this time, Nathanson had decided that abortion could be justified only when the life of the mother was threatened. The same year that *Aborting America* was published, Nathanson stopped performing abortions. He had always believed that a society's morality must be judged by its treatment of the weak and defenseless, and his own early work for abortion reform had been inspired by a concern for the poor. But ultrasound technology had revealed to him an even more vulnerable class: the unborn.

THE SILENT SCREAM

One day, Nathanson had a brainstorm. Since ultrasound could reveal the baby in womb, it could also be used to witness an abortion. He asked a colleague who was performing several abortions a day to put an ultrasound device on a few of the patients and, with their permission, tape the procedure.

Nathanson knew quite well what happened in an abortion. Yet when he saw abstract concepts transformed into vivid images— when he actually witnessed tiny bodies being torn limb from limb—he was startled and revolted. Even more sickening, the ultrasound showed the babies desperately trying to wriggle away from the suction apparatus. One twelve-week fetus continued to struggle even after it had been severely maimed, opening his mouth in what looked horrifyingly like a scream of fear and pain.[4]

Nathanson made the tape of the twelve-week fetus into a film and titled it *The Silent Scream.*[5] When it was released in 1985, it instantly transformed the nature of the abortion debate. Pro-abortion forces raged, accusing Nathanson and the producers of faking the footage. When the authenticity of the tape was confirmed, they switched tactics and sidetracked the discussion into the question of whether a fetus is capable of feeling pain during an abortion—as the fetus so clearly appeared to in the film. Without proposing any theological position, Nathanson had forced abortion supporters to acknowledge that abortion is about taking human life.

ANOTHER SILENT SCREAM

At the same time, an internal "silent scream" began to dominate Bernard Nathanson's own life. Troubling questions played and replayed in his mind: How could I have been so blind to the true nature of abortion? How could I have presided over mass slaughter? And with such a crassly utilitarian attitude, as if it were nothing more than a matter of professional competence?

He began a profound examination of conscience, digging into his past to uncover the source of his skewed ideas. His father, Joseph Nathanson, a wealthy doctor, had sent him to Hebrew school while at the same time ridiculing the spiritual lessons taught there. Although the older Nathanson dismissed the religious claims of Judaism as superstition, he wanted his son to embrace Judaism as an ethnic identity. Joseph Nathanson, having escaped the poverty he grew up in, was driven by materialism.

Now, looking back, Bernard Nathanson realized he had learned
one overwhelming lesson from his father: *Don't let anyone get in
your way.*

And he had learned the lesson well. He had even consigned
not one, but two of his own children to death. The first time an
unwanted pregnancy threatened to "get in the way," he was in
medical school, and he gave his pregnant lover the money to get an
illegal abortion. The second time was in the mid-sixties, when he
was between marriages and his womanizing resulted in an inconve-
nient pregnancy. That was the abortion he had performed himself.

Like his father, Bernard Nathanson had grown materialistic
and ruthlessly ambitious. His first marriage had been fashionable
and without substance. His second marriage gave him his son,
Joey, but Nathanson had neglected the boy for an ever more fran-
tic swirl of professional activities and appointments. His idea of
parenting was to send his son to expensive private schools. After
that marriage ended, he played the swinging bachelor. Eventually,
he destroyed his third marriage as well.

He had lived an "unspeakably shallow" life, as he wrote later,
acquiring lavish homes, trendy autos, trophy wives, wine cellars,
and horses. Then, as he aged, he sought desperately to recover
his youth through cosmetic surgery, bodybuilding, and fashions
designed for college kids. "I was dwelling in the suzerainty of
the demons of sin," he wrote, "oblivious to all but the seemingly
endless carnival of pleasures, the party that never ends (or so the
demons would have you believe)."[6]

But the heaviest baggage Nathanson carried was abortion.
Abortion, abortion, abortion. How ironic that his one great
humanitarian cause had turned out to be nothing less than mass
slaughter. Nathanson found himself face-to-face with guilt. Real
guilt. Not a passing feeling of shame or a confused embarrass-
ment, but a brutal, crushing, dogged knowledge of his own evil.
He was a charred ruin.

Off and on during the late 1980s, Nathanson contemplated suicide. He would awake from fitful dreams at four or five o'clock in the morning, feeling as if he were being strangled by some nameless dread. His grandfather and sister had committed suicide, and he found himself asking, "Would the people closest to me find my death a relief?"

He turned to what he called the "literature of sin." He read St. Augustine's *Confessions* repeatedly and absorbed books by Kierkegaard, Tillich, Niebuhr, and Dostoyevsky—works that described the soul's tormented search for answers to guilt. "Your beauty drew me to you," Augustine wrote. "I had no doubt at all that you were the one to whom I would cling, only . . . my inner self was a house divided against itself."[7] Augustine wanted to turn to God, but he couldn't bring himself to do it. Nathanson's own cry echoed Augustine's agonizing meditations.

But was Augustine's ultimate solution available to him? Could Nathanson accept Christianity? Ever since his childhood, he had associated the name of Jesus Christ with the long history of Christian persecution of the Jewish people. So instead of turning to Christianity, he sought relief in therapy, self-help books, antidepressant drugs, counseling, and a hodgepodge of spiritual approaches, from theosophy to Swedenborgianism. All to no avail.

"I felt the burden of sin growing heavier and more insistent," Nathanson wrote. "I [had] such heavy moral baggage to drag into the next world. . . . I [was] afraid."[8]

WAS THERE HOPE?

Then, in 1989, Nathanson attended a pro-life rally in New York City to gather data for an article he was writing on the ethics of abortion clinic protests. Forbidden to participate himself because of a court order stemming from earlier protests (he had been convicted of trespassing), he stood apart as an objective observer. And what he saw there finally broke through his defenses.

The pro-life activists seemed to have an otherworldly peace. "With pro-choicers hurling the most fulsome epithets at them, the police surrounding them, the media openly unsympathetic to their cause, the federal judiciary fining and jailing them, and municipal officials threatening them—all through it they sat smiling, quietly praying, singing, confident," Nathanson wrote. They exhibited an "intensity of love and prayer that astonished me."

It was only then, with this vivid image of love pressing in on him, that Nathanson began "for the first time in my entire adult life . . . to entertain seriously the notion of God."[9]

Almost immediately, he turned from the literature of sin to the literature of conversion, especially to *Pillar of Fire,* an autobiography detailing the conversion of Karl Stern, one of Nathanson's former teachers. As a medical student, Nathanson had been fascinated by Stern, the leading figure in McGill University's department of psychiatry. In his book, Stern described his long intellectual journey from nominal Judaism to a highly intellectual and devout Christianity. In retrospect, Nathanson realized that Stern's religious beliefs were what had transformed mere medical technique into medical *care.* Nathanson had been drawn to Stern's methods without understanding their inspiration.

That's the kind of transformation I want in my own life and practice, he thought.

In 1993, Nathanson shut down his practice to pursue advanced studies in bioethics, first at Georgetown University, then at Vanderbilt, where bioethics students were allowed to incorporate religious studies in their programs. He also sought counsel from rabbis, for he had come to the point where he believed he would meet his Creator someday. How could he enter the presence of a just God? The rabbis taught that one can atone through performing good works, through hearing the declaration of God's forgiveness of Israel at Yom Kippur. But how, Nathanson wondered, can one know forgiveness personally and individually? How could he himself be delivered from death—the death of all the lives he had taken and the death of his own soul?

In the dim hours of early morning he sometimes felt that he had already entered a hell marked "No Exit," that his "good intentions" had led him to become, in his words, the "Mayor of Hell."[10] His own sense of justice haunted him. He stood condemned in his own eyes. Was there any hope for him?

CHAPTER 9

IN SEARCH OF REDEMPTION

As you read, keep the following questions in mind:
- What is the great human predicament?
- In what ways does advertising entice us with the promise of redemption?

One day in late autumn 1996, my secretary informed me of a surprising phone call. Dr. Bernard Nathanson was inviting my wife and me to his baptism at St. Patrick's Cathedral, with Cardinal John O'Connor presiding.

I was stunned. "Are you sure you've got the right name?" I asked. "Bernard Nathanson?"

"That's it," she said with a smile.

I had known that Nathanson was interested in Christianity; in fact, the two of us had been trying to meet for some time, but we had been unable to coordinate our schedules, and I had no idea he had come so far. I confess I experienced a twinge of disappointment that I hadn't introduced him to the Baptist tradition, yet I was overjoyed to learn that the man who had once been the nation's leading abortionist was now a Christian. It was an invitation I could not refuse.

A few weeks later, on a cold December morning, Patty and I stepped along briskly as we walked the few blocks from our Manhattan hotel to St. Patrick's for the 7:30 service. We had been told to go to the back entrance of the massive cathedral, where we were greeted by a smiling young man in a black coat and a broad-brimmed black hat. He introduced himself as Father John McCloskey and led us down a few steps to a basement entrance.

I knew of McCloskey, a charismatic young priest who had a powerful student ministry at Princeton University. He had also given Nathanson the good news of forgiveness that he so desperately sought and had guided him into the Christian faith.

Father McCloskey led us to a small basement chapel, chilly and damp, where about fifty people were seated on folding chairs. No pomp or ceremony, just a group of believers surrounding a small altar. We could have been the first-century church, gathered in the catacombs, about to witness the baptism of a new believer in the name of the resurrected Christ.

Standing before the altar, Cardinal O'Connor gave a short welcoming homily. Then Nathanson was escorted forward by a young woman whom I immediately recognized as Joan Andrews (now Joan Andrews Bell). *How God delights in ironies,* I thought. Andrews was a former nun who had spent five years in a Florida prison for nonviolent resistance at abortion clinics. In the prison, thieves and murderers came and went, while Joan—her parole consistently denied by a stubborn judge—sat silently in her cell praying. Eventually most people forgot who Joan Andrews was, and she might have wondered if her act of protest had been worth the cost. But God uses every act of faithful obedience, and here she was, guiding one of the world's leading abortionists to the baptismal font.

It was a striking moment of spiritual victory. Most of the time, we Christians fight in the trenches, seeing only the bloody warfare around us. But every so often God permits us a glimpse of the real victory. This was one of those rare, illuminating moments, as we watched Bernard Nathanson—a Jew by birth, a man who had been an atheist by conviction and a brilliant but amoral doctor by profession—kneeling before the cross of Christ.

My mind flashed back to a day three months earlier when I had joined a group of religious leaders to walk the corridors of Congress and plead with senators to override President Clinton's veto of a ban on partial-birth abortions. During the roll call of votes, I sat in the gallery, watching and praying. The atmosphere that day was unusually solemn; the senators seemed to move about the chamber in slow motion. The only sound was the secretary calling the roll, followed by "yea" or "nay" responses.

Suddenly the shrill cry of a baby pierced the eerie silence . . . probably the child of a tourist visiting the Capitol building. Was it my imagination, or did some of the senators turn ashen? The sound of a live baby in that chamber was a vivid reminder of what was at stake in this crucial vote.

Yet it made no difference. The vote to override failed.

Dejected, ashamed for my country, I made my way through the crowds and down one floor to the marble reception room just off the Senate chambers. There I saw Kate Michelman, a leader of the pro-abortion forces, and a group of her cohorts celebrating—embracing, cheering, and exchanging high fives. The scene struck me as macabre. Here were well-dressed, professional women celebrating the right to continue an utterly barbaric practice: a procedure in which a baby is removed from the birth canal backward, all except for its head, then the base of the skull is punctured and the baby's brains are sucked out.

That day, the pro-choicers won an important political victory. And yet it paled in comparison to what Patty and I were witnessing, just three months later, at Bernard Nathanson's baptismal service. There before our eyes was the real victory: God's ultimate triumph over sin through Christ's sacrifice on the cross.

After the baptism, our small group gathered in an Irish pub on Second Avenue. Bernard Nathanson, Father McCloskey, Joan

Andrews, several priests (most of whom also had been imprisoned for nonviolent demonstrations against abortion), and other Right to Life activists filled the half-dozen tables, ordering late breakfasts of bagels and scrambled eggs. Speaking softly and with deep feeling, Nathanson thanked everyone for coming.

"All I could think about while I was kneeling at the altar was my bar mitzvah," he said. "That day I was so afraid." He hesitated, then looked up. "Today I felt all that fear fall away. I experienced sheer grace."

THE GREAT HUMAN PREDICAMENT

Bernard Nathanson had been redeemed. He was a new man, taking his first tentative steps into a new world of faith and hope, his fears relieved, his tormented soul transformed, and the most vexing questions of life answered. As I listened to him speak, I shivered with wonder at the transformation that can take place in the human soul. Dorothy Sayers, mystery writer and friend of C. S. Lewis, coined the phrase "The dogma is the drama," meaning that the Christian teaching on salvation has all the artistic elements of a great story.[1] Indeed, it is the best story ever told. No novelist, no playwright, no movie scriptwriter has ever come up with a plot line so compelling. And it is reenacted every time a person stops running from the Hound of Heaven and gives in to his relentless pursuit of love.

Not all of us, of course, are driven to the depths of despair that Nathanson was. Yet all human beings yearn, deep in their hearts, for deliverance from sin and guilt. Many try to suppress the longing, to rationalize it away, to mute it with lesser answers. But ultimately, it is impossible to evade. This is the great human predicament: Sooner or later, even the most decent among us know that there is a rottenness at our core. We all long to find freedom from our guilt and failures, to find some greater meaning and purpose in life, to know that there is hope.

This need for salvation has been imprinted on the human soul since the first couple went astray in the Garden. The desire is universal, and every religion and worldview offers some form of redemption. For the Buddhist, it is nirvana; for the Jew, it is the atonement of good works; for the Muslim, it may be heaven after the perilous walk across the sword of judgment.

But religions and philosophies are not the only ones offering redemption. Any belief system in the marketplace of ideas, any movement that attracts followers, anything that has the power to grab people's hearts and win their allegiance does so because it taps into their deepest longings. And those longings are, ultimately, religious.

Just as every worldview offers an answer to the question of how we got here (creation), and an analysis of the basic human dilemma (the Fall), so every worldview offers a way to solve that dilemma (redemption). But which offer of redemption is true? Which gives a genuine answer to the human dilemma? And which ones are crass counterfeits?

MORALITY PLAYS FOR TODAY

The siren that calls many people today is the one that claimed Bernard Nathanson's heart and soul for so long: the belief that the object of life is material gain, that achievement and advancement and sensual pleasure are "all there is." America has a highly developed, technologically advanced industry—the advertising industry—designed to entice us with the promise of redemption through materialism and commercialism.

Every time we turn on the television set or open a magazine or newspaper, <u>we are bombarded with the gospel of commercialism: that for every need, every insecurity, every worry, there is a product for sale that can satisfy our need, pump up our self-esteem, soothe our worry.</u> Advertisers devote huge budgets to hiring psychologists to probe the human psyche and pinpoint our deepest needs and longings. Then they craft seductive images and phrases designed to hook us, to beguile us into thinking that buying their product will satisfy those fundamental needs.

And since those deepest needs are religious, what ads really trade on is the universal longing for redemption.

This is no accident. According to sociologist James Twitchell, in his book *Adcult U.S.A.,* many of America's early advertisers were Christians, often sons of clergymen. As they developed the art of modern advertising, they simply translated their understanding of spiritual need into the commercial arena. The spiritual sequence of sin-guilt-redemption became the psychological sequence of problem-anxiety-resolution. That's why the typical television commercial is, in Twitchell's words, "a morality play for our time."[2] We see a man or woman in distress. He has a headache; she has a cold. A second figure appears on the screen promising relief, testifying to the power of the product being advertised. The seeker tries the product, and, hallelujah, the problem is solved. Life is blissful. From on high, the disembodied voice of an announcer presses home the advantages of the product.

"The powerful allure of religion and advertising is the same," Twitchell concludes. Both reassure us that "we will be rescued."[3]

This message takes various forms. Sometimes ads trade on themes of personal faith, with slogans such as "I found it!" "It's the right thing." "Something to believe in." Others offer a veiled substitute for a personal relationship with the divine: "Me and my RC" "You're in good hands." Still others suggest the blessings of the Promised Land: "We bring good things to life." "Be all you can be." Finally, some ads exploit the rhetoric of religious gratitude: "Thank you, TastyKakes." "Thanks, Delco." "I love what you do for me."[4]

In recent years we've even seen religion itself pop up in ads. After all, what is deeper than the need for God? Take an appeal to status or pleasure, combine it with an appeal to religion—or turn pleasure itself into a religion—and the allure is all but irresistible.

Picture this: A family battles desperately as floodwaters threaten to wash away their home. With the house on the verge of collapse, the father cries out for help. And behold, the heavens open and a giant hand descends from the sky to rescue the family from disaster.

Deliverance by God? No. Deliverance by Allstate Insurance Company. The ad co-opts the universal longing for security, which is, at core, a religious longing. One almost expects to see the family offer up a prayer: "We thank you, Allstate, for your protection in times of trouble."

Then there's the ad that shows a young woman in church "confessing" her miserly ways. "It's not a sin to be frugal," the preacher reassures her. And the young woman is released from guilt to enjoy her sporty but economical new Chevy Cavalier.

One IBM ad shows Catholic nuns walking to vespers while whispering about surfing the Net. Another IBM ad shows Buddhist monks meditating telepathically about Lotus Notes. Gatorade features Michael Jordan running in Tibet and meeting an Eastern holy man, who intones, "Life is a sport. Drink it up." Snickers shows a football team inviting a Catholic priest to bless the team, followed by a rabbi, a Native American, a Buddhist, and a long line of other spiritual leaders. "Not going anywhere for a while?" says the tag line. "Grab a Snickers." A Volvo ad shows a man being bathed in flowing, crystal-clear water. As he looks skyward, a soothing, ethereal voice says, "Volvo, it can help save your soul."[5]

Clearly, advertisers are attuned to the human yearning for salvation—and eager to exploit it. Novelist John Updike compares the effort put into commercials with the fanatical care medieval monks devoted to decorating sacred manuscripts. The goal of all

this advertising artistry is "to persuade us that a certain beer, or
candy bar, or insurance company, or oil-based conglomerate is,
like the crucified Christ, . . . the gateway to the good life." Modern advertising makes "every living room a cathedral," and places
within it, every six minutes or so, the icons of modern culture—
"votive objects as luxurious and loving as a crucifixion by
Grünewald or a pietà by Michelangelo."[6]

Calvin Coolidge, our thirtieth president, once told the American Association of Advertising Agencies that "advertising ministers to the spiritual side of trade." It is part of the "greater work of
the regeneration and redemption of mankind."[7] Regeneration?
Redemption? Through advertising, the "religion" of appetite
and ego gratification is offered to us as a solution to the human
dilemma, a comfort in our insecurities, a way of salvation. The
most advanced tools of communication and persuasion are being
used to press us into the service of America's most popular deity,
the idol of consumerism.

But as Bernard Nathanson would tell you, material goods and
consumer items offer no comfort when one enters the dark night
of the soul. As some people have said, the poor are better off than
the rich because the poor still think money will buy happiness;
the rich know better.

Practicing the religion of consumerism is like drinking salt
water: The more you drink, the thirstier you get. There is never
enough wealth and power to satisfy, never enough material possessions to blot out guilt. And no matter how pleasant or attractive
such things can make our brief existence here on earth, they cannot carry us beyond. For the old adage is apt: You can't take it
with you.

Though consumerism is America's favorite substitute religion,
it is not the only one. Others have proven equally seductive . . .
and even more destructive.

*One of the most dangerous errors
instilled into us by the nineteenth-
century progressive optimism is the
idea that civilization is automatically
bound to increase and spread. The
lesson of history is the opposite.*

C. S. LEWIS

CHAPTER 10

DOES IT LIBERATE?

As you read, keep the following questions in mind:

- How did Hegel change the "ladder model" of history?
  What was the significance of this paradigm shift?

- Trace the biblical parallels—creation, paradise, fall,
  bondage, redemption—in Marxist philosophy.

When Diane went off to college in 1967, she also went off the
deep end. Within weeks she was smoking pot, flouting her childhood faith, and mouthing slogans about women's liberation.

Today, Diane has returned to her Christian faith and no longer
calls herself a feminist. "I got tired of being a victim," she explains.
"I used to read feminist books by the armload. Then one day it
hit me. All those books were the same! Every problem a woman
might have was explained by saying that someone, somewhere
had done her wrong—as if women were weak, passive creatures.
It was pathetic."

Diane has changed her mind, but millions still march behind
the banner of women's liberation—along with a host of other
liberation ideologies. Across the nation, groups gather around
ideologies of gender, race, and sexual orientation, seething with
rage over alleged oppressions of one kind or another.

To understand the appeal these groups exert, we need to understand their underlying worldview. According to these groups,

what is the human dilemma, the source of suffering and injustice? Oppression by whites or males or heterosexuals or some other group. What is the solution, the way to justice and peace? Raising our consciousness and rising up against the oppressor. Thus, the promise of liberation is ultimately a promise of redemption.

All the liberation ideologies in the marketplace of ideas today are variations on a single theme that has been pervasive in Western thought since the nineteenth century: that history is moving forward toward a glorious consummation. This is sometimes dubbed the "myth of progress," or, in the words of British philosopher Mary Midgley, "the Escalator Myth," and it is a secularization of the Christian teaching of divine providence. Whereas Christianity teaches that history is moving toward the kingdom of God, the Escalator Myth reassures us that we are evolving toward an earthly utopia that is the product of human effort and ingenuity.[1]

Along with the denial of sin, the idea of inevitable progress has fueled the great utopian movements that we traced in the previous section. This idea first took hold through the work of the nineteenth-century German philosopher Georg Friedrich Hegel. Until that time, the world had been pictured as a static ladder of life. Everything had its niche on a rung on this great ladder—from rocks to plants to animals to humans to angels to God himself. But Hegel did something entirely new, something really breathtaking. He tilted the ladder of life on its side, so that instead of being a list of all the things that exist in the world at any one time, it became a series of *stages* through which the world passes during the course of history. Thus the ladder was transformed into a dynamic series of steps: Everything moves from one rung to the next in an endless progress toward perfection.[2]

As a result of Hegel's influence, everything was seen as subject to evolution—not just living things but also customs, cultures, and concepts. The universe was thought to be in a process of constant change, caught up in a great transformation from primitive beginnings to some exalted future. In every field, from biology to anthropology, from law to sociology, there was a fevered search for "laws of development" that would reveal the pattern of history and the direction of evolution, providing people with guidance on how to live in accord with that great movement toward a better world. There was great optimism that the best human minds could uncover the laws of progress and lead us forward into utopia—a substitute vision of heaven. Philosophers and thinkers began vying with one another to be the one to unveil the path to the earthly heaven, the means of redemption.

The Escalator Myth took various forms, some of which will be the topics of the following chapters, as we discuss the theme of redemption.

NEO-MARXISM IS ALIVE AND WELL

Hegel's best-known disciple was Karl Marx, and Marxism is best understood as a prime example of the Escalator Myth—of an effort by the modern mind to secularize the kingdom of God, to create a purely human heaven here on earth. Marxism may be discredited as a political theory in most parts of the world today, but it lives on in updated form in various liberation movements, as we noted at the beginning of this chapter. The cast has changed, but the plot is the same.

In the classic Marxist drama of history, the oppressed were the proletariat (urban factory workers); in the newer multiculturalist ideologies, the oppressed are women, blacks, or homosexuals. In classic Marxism, the proletariat will rise up against their oppressors—the capitalists; in the updated forms, people of various colors and genders are likewise called to harness their rage and do battle against their oppressors—usually white male heterosexuals.

The politically correct campus today offers countless variations on the Marxist theme, but the common core of all these variations is revealed by the way they overlap and complement one another. The University of California at Santa Barbara offers a course listed as Black Marxism, linking Marxism and black liberation. Brown University connects black and homosexual liberation in a course called Black Lavender: Study of Black Gay/Lesbian Plays. UCLA relates Hispanic ethnicity with homosexuality in a course listed as Chicana Lesbian Literature. Villanova combines feminism with environmentalism in a course titled Eco-feminism. And Stanford University mixes everything in a single cauldron with a course its catalog lists as Women of Color: The Intersection of Race, Ethnicity, Class, and Gender. As a result of this massive politicization of education, college students are being taught to apply Marxist categories to law, politics, education, family studies, and many other fields.

What all this means is that Marxism, though largely discredited as a political ideology, is still very much alive and well in Western intellectual life. Reborn as multiculturalism and political correctness, it remains one of the most widespread and influential forms of counterfeit salvation. Government-mandated group rights and other outgrowths of multiculturalism are even being read into the U.S. Constitution, so that though original Marxism never took over our nation, this reborn Marxism may yet do so.

A GULAG IN THE END

While Karl Marx hunched over his books in the British Museum in the mid–nineteenth century, feverishly philosophizing, what he eventually came up with was a full-blown alternative religion. In the beginning was a creator: namely, matter itself. In Marxism the universe is a self-originating, self-operating machine, generating its own power and running by its own internal force toward a final goal—the classless, communistic society. Marx's disciple, Lenin, stated the doctrine in explicitly religious language: "We may regard the material and cosmic world as the supreme being, as the cause of all causes, as the creator of heaven and earth."[3]

Redemption Story

Marxism's counterpart to the Garden of Eden is the state of primitive communism. And the original sin was the creation of private property and the division of labor, which caused humanity to fall from its early state of innocence into slavery and oppression. From this follow all the subsequent evils of exploitation and class struggle.

In this drama, redemption is wrought by reversing the original sin: destroying the private ownership of the means of production. And the redeemer is the proletariat, who will rise up against the capitalist oppressors. In the words of historian Robert Wesson, "The savior-proletariat [will] by its suffering redeem mankind and bring the Kingdom of Heaven on earth."[4]

The Day of Judgment, in Marxist theology, is the day of revolution, when the evil bourgeoisie will be damned.[5] It is significant that Marx called not for repentance but for revolution. Why? Because, like Rousseau, he regarded humanity as inherently good. He believed that evil and greed arise from the economic structures of society (private property), and therefore they can be eliminated by a social revolution that destroys the old economic system and institutes a new one.

Finally, like all religions, Marxism has an eschatology (a doctrine of the final events of history). In Christianity, the end of time is when the original perfection of God's creation will be restored, and sin and pain will be no more. In Marxism, the end of history is when the original communism will be restored and class conflict will be no more. Paradise will be ushered in by the efforts of human beings whose consciousness has been raised. Marx looked forward to this inevitable consummation of history as eagerly as any Christian anticipates the Second Coming.

"Marxism is a secularized vision of the kingdom of God," writes theology professor Klaus Bockmuehl. "It is the kingdom of man. The race will at last undertake to create for itself that 'new earth in which righteousness dwells.' "[6] Marxism promises to solve the human dilemma and create the New Man living in an ideal society.

These religious elements explain Marxism's puzzling powers of endurance. Most of Marx's specific theories have failed spectacularly, and his promise of a classless society has never come to pass, despite countless Marxist-inspired revolutions around the globe.[7]

Why, then, is Marxism still so popular? Why do so many liberation movements today adopt Marxist categories and analysis? Why have multiculturalism and political correctness cut a huge swath across the university campus, sweeping up students like Diane and teaching them to view the world through the lens of aggrieved self-righteousness? Precisely because Marxism aims at an essentially religious need, tapping into humanity's hunger for redemption.

Marx himself knew he was offering a militantly atheistic counterpart to Christianity. "Marx was confirmed at fifteen and for a time seems to have been a passionate Christian," says historian Paul Johnson. But ultimately he rejected the biblical God, denouncing religion as "the illusory sun around which man revolves, until he begins to revolve around himself."[8]

Autonomous Goal

Marx's ultimate goal was autonomy. He wrote: "A *being* only considers himself independent when he stands on his own feet; and he only stands on his own feet when he owes his *existence* to himself." But a person cannot be independent if he is the creation of a personal God, for then "he lives by the grace of another."[9] So Marx determined to become his own master, a god to himself.

This is the root of Marxism, and it is the point where we must begin to critique it. How plausible is this insistence on absolute autonomy? Ironically, Marx himself admitted that it is highly *im*plausible. Belief in a creator, he acknowledged, is "very difficult to dislodge from popular consciousness"; at the same time, to most people the notion of absolute autonomy is "incomprehensible." Why? "Because it contradicts everything *tangible* in practical life."[10] In other words, in real life it is obvious that we are *not* completely autonomous. We do not create ourselves, and we cannot exist completely on our own. We are finite, contingent, dependent beings—tiny specks within a vast universe, a mere eddy within the ever flowing stream of history.

The conclusion is that Marx's worldview is fatally flawed; it does not match up with reality. And Marx himself admitted as much in acknowledging that his philosophy "contradicts everything" in "practical life." Marx is a living example of the apostle Paul's description of unbelievers: They *know* the truth, and still they suppress it (See Rom. 1:18-32).

As a young man, Marx wrote poetry, much of it dwelling on themes of rage, destruction, and savagery. One of his surviving pieces includes these lines:

> Then I will wander godlike and victorious
> Through the ruins of the world
> And, giving my words an active force,
> I will feel equal to the creator.[11]

Here he reveals the ultimate religious motivation behind his philosophy: to be equal to the Creator, to give his own words the active force of God's creative words.

Disastrous Ends

Marx's self-deification has had disastrous results for millions, leading to war, massacre, and labor camps. "Apply Marxism in any country you want, you will always find a Gulag in the end," says

French philosopher Bernard-Henri Levi, himself a former Marxist.[12] Because <u>revolutionaries are confident that the next stage in history will automatically represent progress,</u> that any change will be for the better, they readily tear down and destroy the existing order—which historically has often meant killing off anyone who resists, from rulers to peasants. Moreover,<u> because Marxism assumes that the reconstruction of social and economic institutions is enough to usher in harmony and peace, it puts no moral restraints on the leaders in the new order.</u> Because it denies the evil in human nature, it does not recognize the need to place checks and balances on the individuals in power, allowing them to accrue absolute power. And we all know what absolute power does.

Marxism is a substitute religion that wreaks devastation and death. And today's liberation movements, which depend heavily on the Marxist worldview, are inherently religious as well. They may have dropped Marx's focus on economics in favor of race or gender or ethnicity, but the basic thought forms remain the same—and they are equally flawed and dangerous.

And for those who really believe in salvation through the Escalator Myth, the sexiest form of liberation is . . . sex itself.

DISCUSSION QUESTIONS

CHAPTER 8

1 Note the title of chapter 8 is "Good Intentions." Discuss Dr. Nathanson's journey in terms of his "intentions." How reliable are good intentions as "guideposts" for moral decision making? Back up your discussion with personal examples.

2 Trace Dr. Nathanson's emotional and spiritual journey. To what unhelpful sources did he turn for "relief"? Through what avenues did he find convincing Christian witness? What does his story encourage you to do?

CHAPTER 9

3 Dr. Nathanson had become a pro-life advocate before becoming a Christian. His conversion did not change his moral belief in that regard. What did his conversion change for him? How and why?

4 What is the great human predicament? In what ways do
people rationalize it away? What "redemption" is offered by
the world's great ancient religions?

5 Contemporary advertising implies that we can buy redemption
along with material goods and services. To illustrate this,
pass out to the group copies of various magazines that run
commercial ads. (Plan for one per person if possible. You
might find old magazines on a library sale rack or in a
recycling Dumpster.) Take a moment to skim the magazines
for examples of ads that rely on redemptive themes. Share
examples with the group, identifying the "theme" of the
message. (If appropriate, tear out the ads and make them into
a collage.)

6 Drawing from your own magazine search and from what you
remember of other advertising media (give examples),
summarize what you see about the "gospel of commercialism."

7 How will what you've learned in this chapter change your
a. buying expectations?

b. shopping habits?

c. parenting?

8 In what healthy and unhealthy ways do we Christians deal with "the universal longing for security"?

CHAPTER 10

9 How is the Escalator Myth related to the ideas of sin, utopia, and evolution? What (and who) is at the heart of the myth of inevitable progress?

10 Make a list of aspects or qualities of your life or household or church community. (Write the list on a flip chart or board, if possible.) Then change the list of qualities into a series of "stages" moving toward perfection. In your small world, what would be the ramifications of this new scheme? Discuss this exercise in light of Hegel's philosophy of history.

11 What are the various contemporary "disguises" of Marxism? What do they have in common? In what ways do they run counter to a biblical view of God, humanity, and history?

12 If the great human dilemma is oppression, "the promise of liberation is ultimately a promise of redemption." Trace the "redemption story" of the Marxist drama of history.

13 Read aloud Romans 1:18-25. What evidence do we have that Marx himself knew that something wasn't right about his philosophy?

14 In talking to secular friends, how can you use the American governmental system of checks and balances as an illustration of the good use and value of foundational Christian truth?

ROLE PLAY

Refer to the directions for role play at the end of session 1 (pp. 40–41).

CONVERSATION STARTER

Assume a neighbor shows you his latest purchase. Like a kid proud of a new bicycle, he says, "I'm a happy man." Walk through a two-way conversation that gets to the key issues in chapter 9. This conversation may be tricky. Think of ways to present truths about spiritual restlessness and false redemptive promises of consumerism without being overly judgmental or "raining on his parade." After all, you don't want him to quit trying to draw you into neighborly conversation. (And the next time you bring home a new lawn mower, maybe you'll want to show off its fancy features.)

CLOSING SUMMARY

What is the one thing you want to remember from what you read (or heard or did) in this session?

Consider sharing this with the group.

SEX, SCIENCE, AND DESPAIR

All the intellectual and cultural breakthroughs of modernity were in some way or other linked to the sexual desires their progenitors knew to be illicit but which they chose nonetheless. Their theories were ultimately rationalizations of the choices they knew to be wrong. E. MICHAEL JONES

CHAPTER 11

SALVATION THROUGH SEX?

As you read, keep the following questions in mind:
- What biblical parallels of redemption can you see in Sanger's philosophy of sexuality?
- What made Kinsey's research unreliable?
- What were the ramifications of Reich's views?
- What is sexual utopianism, and where do we still see evidence of it?

In his 1967 novel *An Exile,* Madison Jones portrays a sheriff who is drawn into adultery with a young woman—and has an experience of transcendence. As they lie in bed together, moonlight falls on colored windowpanes in the turret above them, reminding the sheriff of a stained-glass window in the church he attended as a child.

"Figured in the glass, in dull colors of blue and yellow and red, was a picture of Jesus blessing the children," Jones writes, "and from that window there fell upon him just such a light as this— a light that was the color of grace, that was God's grace itself descending through the window upon them all."

Gazing at the young woman sleeping beside him, the sheriff muses, "It was grace, the preacher had said, that made sinless, sinful man; and there he sat bathed in it. New-born in grace.

Was it not strange that now, with the sweat of his sin barely yet dry upon him, he should feel as he had felt then?"

Strange indeed. For the sheriff's relationship with this young woman is solely sexual. He does not love her, and she does not love him. In fact, as the reader later discovers, she has been coerced into the relationship by her father, who is engaged in criminal activity and hopes to corrupt the sheriff. Still, this loveless, utilitarian, purely physical encounter is portrayed as an avenue for a religious experience.

"Like new, [the sheriff] thought: purged of the old body and the old mind. So this was grace. . . ."[1] The sheer physical act of intercourse, even in a sinful, loveless relationship, is portrayed paradoxically as a means of grace.

Medieval mystics used meditation and self-denial to achieve transcendence and to commune with the sacred; modernists use sex.

Sex is a vital part of God's created order, a sacred part of the marriage covenant; and our sexual nature is a good gift from God. But for many modern thinkers, sexuality has become the basis for an entire worldview, the source of ultimate meaning and healing, a means of redemption. Sex has been exalted to the means of raising ourselves to the next level of evolution, creating a new kind of human nature and an advanced civilization. In short, sexuality has been transformed into another version of the Escalator Myth.

Where do these near mystical ideas of sexuality come from? In large measure, they stem from Rousseau, who taught that human nature was good and that evil was the result of the constraints of civilization, with its moral rules and social conventions. In the nineteenth century, Freud attributed neurosis to the constraints of moral rules and the guilt they produce. Then, as science learned more about the physiology of sexuality—for example, the action of the glands—these same ideas were dressed up in scientific garb.

SANGER'S SALVATION

For example, in the early twentieth century Margaret Sanger, who is generally remembered as an early champion of birth control, taught a broad philosophy of sexuality, a philosophy reinforced by science. She contended that sexual restraint suppresses the activity of the sex glands and thus injures health and dulls the intellect. Thus science itself, she argued, supports sexual liberation.

The drama of history, by Sanger's account, consists of a struggle to free our bodies and minds from the constraints of morality, the prohibitions that distort and impoverish human nature. She adamantly opposed "the 'moralists' who preached abstinence, self-denial, and suppression," and described Christian ethics as "the cruel morality of self-denial and 'sin.' " She hoped to replace it with her own morality of sexual liberation, promising that the release of sexual energies was "the only method" by which a person could find "inner peace and security and beauty."[2] And also the only method for overcoming social ills: "Remove the constraints and prohibitions which now hinder the release of inner energies, [and] most of the larger evils of society will perish."[3]

What Sanger offered was nothing less than a doctrine of salvation in which morality is the root of all evil and free sexual expression is the path to redemption. She even resorted to religious language, calling on a sexual elite to "remove the moral taboos that now bind the human body and spirit, free the individual from the slavery of tradition, and above all answer their unceasing cries for knowledge that would make possible their self-direction and salvation."[4] Salvation? In another passage, she promises that men and women will literally become geniuses through "the removal of physiological and psychological inhibitions and constraints which makes possible the release and channeling of the primordial inner energies of man into full and divine expression."[5] Divine? Here's a new twist on the serpent's promise in Eden: It's not eating the fruit from the tree in the Garden that will make us godlike; it's the release of sexual energies.

Sanger's philosophy is simply another version of the Escalator Myth in which sexual freedom is the means to transform human nature and create the New Man. It is in our power to "remodel the [human] race" and create "a real civilization," to "transmute and sublimate the everyday world into a realm of beauty and joy," she wrote euphorically. And she resorts again to religious language: "Through sex, mankind may attain the great spiritual illumination which will transform the world, which will light up the only path to an earthly paradise."[6]

KINSEY'S RESEARCH

One of Sanger's contemporaries, Alfred Kinsey, was equally influential in shaping sexual mores and sex-education theories, particularly with his books *Sexual Behavior in the Human Male* and *Sexual Behavior in the Human Female*, published in the 1940s.[7] Kinsey's impact was due in part to the pose he struck as an objective scientist, tabulating what Americans did in their bedrooms. But the truth is that he was neither objective nor scientific. Like Sanger, he was committed to an ideology that defined morality as a harmful force to be opposed and that elevated sexuality into a means of salvation.

To liberate sex from morality, Kinsey reduced sex to the sheer biological act of physical orgasm. He then claimed that all orgasms are morally equivalent—whether between married or unmarried persons, between people of the same or the opposite sex, between adults or children, even between humans and animals. His model was the animal world. Kinsey was a devout Darwinian who believed that since humans evolved from animals, there are no significant differences between them. He liked to talk about "the human animal," and if a particular behavior could be found among animals, he considered it normative for humans as well. For example, Kinsey claimed that certain mammals are observed to have sexual contact between males, and even across species; therefore, he concluded, both homosexuality and bestiality are "part of the normal mammalian picture" and are acceptable behavior for humans.[8]

So eager was Kinsey to drive home his philosophy that he employed highly unscientific research methods, such as relying on unrepresentative samples that included a disproportionate percentage of sex offenders and other deviants. It is hardly scientific to use such skewed samples to define "normal" sexuality, and yet, as biographer James Jones documents, Kinsey persistently studied people who were on the margins, or even beyond the pale, in their sexual behavior: homosexuals, sadomasochists, voyeurs, exhibitionists, pedophiles, transsexuals, and fetishists.[9]

Kinsey remained undeterred by criticism, however, for his sexual views were not based ultimately on science but on an intensely held personal belief system. In the words of Stanford professor Paul Robinson, a sympathetic critic, Kinsey viewed history "as a great moral drama, in which the forces of science competed with those of superstition for the minds and hearts of men."[10] By "superstition," Kinsey meant religion and its moral prescriptions. Kinsey sometimes spoke as if the introduction of Bible-based sexual morality was *the* watershed in human history, a sort of "Fall" from which we must be redeemed. For Kinsey, sexual expression was the means of saving human nature from the oppression of religion and morality.

REICH'S REFLEX

Another major influence on American sexual attitudes was Austrian psychologist Wilhelm Reich, who became something of a cult figure in the 1960s. His contribution was the search for the "ultimate orgasm," which quickly became one of the fads of the human potential movement. Reich taught that nearly everyone is in some degree neurotic and that every neurosis is in turn a symptom of sexual failure. Therefore, the answer to all human dysfunction is to develop "the capacity for surrender to the flow of biological energy without any inhibition, the capacity for complete discharge of all dammed-up sexual excitation through involuntary pleasurable contractions of the body."[11] Reich believed that human beings are nothing more than biological creatures and that redemption comes through complete immersion in the sexual reflex.

The enemy in Reich's sexual Eden is, once again, traditional religion and morality, that "murderous philosophy" that creates guilt, distorts our drives, and gives rise to personality disorders.[12] He insisted that since nature knows nothing of morality, any moral restraints on the sexual impulse work like a slow poison on the entire personality. In a book aptly titled *Salvation through Sex*, psychiatrist Eustace Chesser says that for Reich, orgasm "is man's only salvation, leading to the Kingdom of Heaven on earth."[13]

RIMMER'S RELIGION

Reich's ideas were incorporated by Robert Rimmer in his provocative novel *The Harrad Experiment*, published in 1966. The book sold three million copies and helped fuel the sexual revolution. For an entire generation of college-educated Americans, it became recommended reading in college courses on marriage and family, and many people credit the book with being instrumental in the sudden merger of male colleges with female colleges and in the creation of coed dormitories.

The novel portrays an experimental college where the students are expected to couple up in various combinations and permutations in order to develop a free and uninhibited approach to sexuality. The philosophy behind this sexual utopia is voiced by the professor who founded the college: "<u>The premise is that man is innately good and can lift himself by his bootstraps into an infinitely better world</u>." How? <u>By sexual liberation</u>. It is the means for taking "one more step up the evolutionary ladder," for "evolving into a new form of man and woman."[14]

Rimmer's view of sex is frankly religious, and he has the professor state openly that intercourse "is actually an act of worship." Or, as he has another character say (quoting philosopher Alan Watts), "What lovers feel for each other in this moment is no other than adoration in the full religious sense. . . . Such adoration which is due God, would indeed be idolatrous were it not that, in that moment, love takes away the illusion and shows the beloved for what he or she in truth is . . . the naturally divine." Sex is portrayed as the path to divinity.[15]

In a postscript added in the 1990 edition of the novel, Rimmer neatly summarizes his religion: "Can we lift ourselves by the bootstraps and create a new kind of society where human sexuality and the total wonder of the human body and the human mind become the new religion—a humanistic religion, without the necessity of a god, because you and I and all the billions who could interact caringly with one another are the only god we need? I think we can."[16]

BEYOND "IGNORANCE"

Sexuality is clearly being presented as more than mere sensual gratification or titillation. It is nothing less than a form of redemption, a means to heal the fundamental flaw in human nature. Only when we see these sexual ideologies as complete worldviews, held with religious fervor, will we understand why Christians and moral conservatives find it so hard to reform sex-education courses in public schools. You won't find contemporary sex educators using words like *salvation;* nonetheless, many hold the same basic assumption that free sexual expression is the means to a full and healthy life.

For example, Mary Calderone, a major architect of contemporary sex education and former executive director of Sex Information and Education Council of the United States (SIECUS), tipped her hand in a 1968 article in which she said that the "real question" facing sex educators is this: "What kind [of person] do we want to produce" to take the place of human nature as we know it today? And "how do we design the production line" to create this advanced creature?[17]

The problem, as Calderone sees it, is that human nature is not evolving as quickly as technology; therefore we must remold human nature itself to fit the modern, ever-changing world. A new stage of evolution is breaking across the horizon, she writes, and the task of educators is to prepare children to step into that new world. To do this, they must pry children away from old views and values, especially from biblical and other traditional forms of sexual morality—for "religious laws or rules about sex were made on the basis of ignorance."[18]

In this new stage of evolution, all currently held values will fall by the wayside, making way for new values based on science alone. Therefore, says Calderone, the best thing we can do for our children is to prepare them to view all notions of right and wrong as tentative, changing, and relative. Then, loosed from the old values, they can be inculcated with the values of a scientifically trained elite (consisting of professionals like herself, of course), who know what makes a human being truly healthy. She calls on schools and churches to use sex education to develop "quality human beings by means of such consciously engineered processes as society's own best minds can blueprint."[19] Here sexual utopianism takes on almost frightening tones, for it ties sex education to a vision of social engineering according to a "blueprint" drawn up by a scientific elite.

SELF-IMPROVEMENT?

When we trace the history of ideas about sexuality, it becomes clear that the founders of sex education never did seek simply to transmit a collection of facts about how our bodies work. Rather, they were evangelists for a utopian worldview, a religion, in which a "scientific" understanding of sexuality is the means for transforming human nature, freeing it from the constraints of morality and ushering in an ideal society. It is another form of the Escalator Myth.

Yet if we examine the lives of these self-appointed prophets, we find little grounds for believing their grandiose promises. Margaret Sanger was married twice and had numerous lovers—or, as she put it, "voluntary mates." She was addicted to the painkiller Demerol and obsessed with numerology, astrology, and psychics in a desperate attempt to find meaning. In her life, sexual liberation was not the high road to salvation that she had promised in her writing.[20]

Kinsey, too, had a secret life we rarely hear about. His goal was "to create his own sexual utopia," says biographer James Jones, and Kinsey built up a select circle of friends and colleagues who committed themselves to his philosophy of total sexual freedom. Since the results were often captured on film, we know that Kinsey and his wife both had sexual relations with a host of male and female staff members and other people. Kinsey was also a masochist, sometimes engaging in bizarre and painful practices.[21]

But Kinsey had an even darker secret. In *Kinsey, Sex, and Fraud*, researcher Judith Reisman argues convincingly that Kinsey's research on child sexual responses could have been obtained only if he or his colleagues were actually engaged in the sexual molestation of children. How else could "actual observations" be made of sexual responses in children age two months to fifteen years old?[22] And this is the man whose ideas have been so influential in shaping American sex education.

Wilhelm Reich's life likewise reveals the flaws in his own philosophy. Reich demanded complete sexual freedom for himself
and conducted multiple affairs, but he couldn't stand the thought
that his wife might live by the same sexual philosophy. His third
wife writes that he was desperately jealous and forbade her from
living as he did.[23] One test of whether a worldview is true is
whether it corresponds to reality: Can we live with it? Obviously
Reich could not.

The truth is that sexual liberation has been no high road to
salvation for those who have worshiped at its shrine. Instead, the
tragic results of sexual licentiousness have spread across our entire
society, producing epidemics of abortion, sexually transmitted
diseases (afflicting one out of four women), and children born out
of wedlock, with all the attendant social pathologies, including
school problems, drug and alcohol abuse, and crime. Yet for many
Americans, sexual liberation remains a cherished right, and the
utopian visions planted by Sanger, Kinsey, Reich, and Calderone
continue to flourish. Their ideas still form the unspoken assumptions in the sex-education curricula used throughout our public
school system.

THE GREAT IRONY

We all base our lives on some vision of ultimate reality that gives
meaning to our individual existence. If we reject God, we will put
something in his place; we will absolutize some part of creation.
That's exactly what has happened with those who look to a sexual
utopia for fulfillment and salvation. Biology takes the place of
God as the ultimate reality, and sex becomes the path to the
divine.

The irony is that those who reject religion most emphatically,
who insist most noisily that they are "scientific," end up promoting what can only be called a religion. In fact, this seems to be a

common malady among those who pride themselves on being scientific. Back in the Age of Reason, science was offered as a substitute for religion. But what few foresaw was that in the process, science would take on the functions of religion. And today, as we shall see, science itself has become one of the most popular forms of redemption.

CHAPTER 1 2

IS SCIENCE OUR SAVIOR?

As you read, keep the following questions in mind:
- What is the myth of science as savior?
- In Comte's view, what were the three stages of social evolution?
- Without moral guidelines, what dangers are inherent in the scientific version of the Escalator Myth?
- Where does the great promise of science and technology lead us?

When the movie *Independence Day* hit the theaters in the late 1990s, many viewers had the feeling they had seen the story somewhere before.[1] In effect, they had. The film was essentially a remake of the 1953 science-fiction classic *War of the Worlds*—but with one significant difference.

While both versions feature aliens invading Earth, in the 1953 movie, scientists come up with a weapon that is eventually destroyed. The panicking population is forced to turn to God; churches are jammed with people praying. What's more, their prayers are answered: The aliens contract earthborn bacteria and suddenly die off. "All that men could do had failed," says a final voice-over; deliverance came from the hand of God alone. The film ends with a scene of people standing on a hillside, singing praise to God.[2]

The contemporary update is quite different—signaling a

dramatic change in American culture within only a few decades. *Independence Day* nods politely in God's direction by showing people praying for help. But real deliverance comes through the deployment of advanced military technology: A few strategically placed bombs blow up the aliens and save the world. *Independence Day* is a celluloid expression of a widespread belief in science and technology as means of salvation.

The outline of this faith is neatly summarized in Daniel Quinn's best-seller *Ishmael,* which features a series of conversations between a disaffected 1960s idealist and a know-it-all gorilla, who offers to explain what's wrong with the world. The problem, says the gorilla, is that Western culture has bought into the myth of science as savior. The myth goes something like this: The universe started out about fifteen billion years ago with the big bang; our solar system was born about seven billion years ago; eventually, life appeared in the chemical broth of the ancient oceans, evolving first into simple microorganisms, then into higher, more complex forms, and finally into human beings. We humans are the apex of evolution, with the intelligence to control nature and bend it to serve our purposes. The solution to our social problems therefore lies in our own hands, through the exertion of human intelligence and ingenuity. Through our ever advancing science and technology, we will save ourselves.[3]

SCIENCE AS SALVATION

Quinn has put his finger squarely on the assumptions that float around in the minds of most Western people, many of whom hold this basic worldview without even realizing that they do. Because the worldview has no name, no label, no church, and no rituals, most people don't identify it as a religion or even as a distinctive belief system. It's simply part of the furniture of the Western mind. Yet it is nothing less than a vision of redemption, a surrogate salvation, a substitute for the kingdom of God, setting up science as the path to utopia.

Looking back over history, we find some of the first dabbling with this notion in the writings of the sixteenth-century scientist Francis Bacon. In a tale titled *New Atlantis,* Bacon depicts an imaginary civilization centered on a gigantic laboratory committed to perpetual progress through science—or, as he quaintly put it, to "the effecting of all things possible."[4]

More influential was the nineteenth-century philosopher Auguste Comte, who is honored today as the founder of sociology. Comte proposed that all societies pass through three stages of social evolution. The most primitive is the theological stage, where people seek supernatural explanations for events; the second is the metaphysical stage, where people explain the world through abstract philosophical concepts; and the highest is the scientific stage, where people find truth through scientific experimentation. Unlike most of his contemporaries, Comte admitted that what he was proposing was essentially a religion. He actually founded a Religion of Humanity, complete with churches and hymns and calendars listing special days for the "saints" of science and philosophy—with himself as the high priest.[5]

But the religion of progress through science really took off after Charles Darwin published his theory of evolution by natural selection. By providing scientific sanction for evolution, Darwin's theory gave enormous impetus to the idea of endless, universal progress.[6] English philosopher Herbert Spencer expanded evolution into a comprehensive philosophy covering all of reality— from stars to societies. In his system, the goal of evolutionary progress is the emergence of human beings, who, in turn, will help produce something new and better for the next stage of evolution. Spencer's gospel of evolution became a secular substitute for Christian hope. As Ian Barbour writes in *Issues in Science and Religion,* "Faith in progress replaced the doctrines of creation

and providence as assurance that the universe is not really purposeless."[7]

Even certain strains of Marxism identify science rather than
revolution as the source of salvation. In the early part of this century, physicist J. D. Bernal predicted that after the triumph of the
proletariat and the rise of the classless society, there was still one
more stage before a real utopia would appear—a stage when a new
"aristocracy of scientific intelligence" would create a world run by
scientific experts. In a burst of enthusiasm, Bernal predicted that
scientists would actually evolve into a new, superhuman race that
would "emerge as a new species and leave humanity behind."[8]

The idea of creating a new and improved race is a key compo-
nent in many forms of scientific utopianism. In the early twentieth
century, after Gregor Mendel's groundbreaking work on genes
was rediscovered, many scientists began to place their hope in a
vision of creating the New Man through genetic engineering. In
the 1930s, the great geneticist H. J. Muller divided the history of
life into three stages: In the first stage, life was completely at the
mercy of the environment; in the second stage, human beings
appeared and reversed that order, learning how to reach out and
control the environment; and in the dawning third stage, humans
would reach inside and control their own nature. Humanity will
"shape itself into an increasingly sublime creation—a being beside
which the mythical divinities of the past will seem more and more
ridiculous," Muller wrote. This godlike being surveys the entire
universe, and, "setting its own marvelous inner powers against the
brute Goliath of the suns and planets, challenges them to contest."[9]

Muller was an excellent scientist, but what he is describing
here is not science. It is science turned into a myth of salvation.

This same myth motivates much of the research done today
in genetic engineering. Nobel prize–winner Francis Crick,
codiscoverer of DNA, writes: "We can expect to see major efforts

to improve the nature of man himself within the next ten thousand years."[10] Some people even believe genetic science will eventually develop "supergenes" to produce human beings with superintelligence or superstrength. This is salvation by genetics—the creation of the New Man by gene manipulation.

REALITY TEST

But will such a salvation really save us? How does this vision of redemption stack up in a test against reality? Not very well.

Science itself gives no moral guidelines for our genetic experimentation. How do we decide which traits we want? Do we want to create a super-Einstein or a super–Mother Teresa, or even a class of subhuman slaves to do our menial work? These questions presuppose a standard of values, which science itself cannot provide.

More important, the sheer attempt to remake human nature genetically would strip people of their dignity and reduce them to commodities. With technology offering greater choice and control over the embryo's traits, having a child could become like purchasing a consumer product. And children themselves may come to be regarded as products that we plan, create, modify, improve, and evaluate according to standards of quality control. What happens if the "product" doesn't meet the parents' standard—if they do not think they're getting their money's worth? Will the child be tossed aside, like an appliance that stops working? As one theologian argues, human beings are "begotten, not made," and if we reverse that—if children become products that we manufacture—we do immeasurable damage to human dignity.[11]

Unfortunately, objections like these are not likely to be raised in a climate where scientists hold a faith in inevitable progress, for the Escalator Myth creates the expectation that change will always be for the better. This explains why some scientists reveal a disturbingly uncritical acceptance of genetic engineering. But clearly, change can be either an improvement or a degeneration. New forms of technology can be used in the service of either good or evil. The faith that we can save ourselves through science can be sustained only if we shut our eyes to the human capacity for barbarism.[12]

Many thoughtful scientists find it hard to go along with such a blind faith. Yet rather than search for another form of salvation, they simply transfer the Escalator Myth to a different galaxy. Because planet Earth is so mired in pollution, war, and other pathologies, they say, we are likely to destroy ourselves before we manage to evolve to a higher stage. For example, Stephen Hawking, author of the best-seller *A Brief History of Time,* warns that evolution will not improve the human race quickly enough to temper our aggression and avoid extinction.[13] Our only hope, then, is to link up with beings elsewhere in the universe—a civilization of extraterrestrials who have themselves successfully evolved to a more advanced stage and can help us.

These are not the rantings of wide-eyed UFO enthusiasts, mind you. Both the federal government and private foundations have poured huge amounts of money into the Search for Extra-Terrestrial Intelligence (SETI), scanning the heavens with powerful radio telescopes in the hope of picking up signals from another civilization. If we ever do discover another civilization in space, says Frank Drake, who heads up the SETI Institute, "it can tell us what we might evolve to, and how far we might evolve." These friendly extraterrestrials might even pass on their technological knowledge, handing over "scientific data which otherwise might take us hundreds of years and vast resources to acquire."[14]

The breathless enthusiasm that often accompanies descriptions of SETI is a dead giveaway that this search for an extraterrestrial solution is at core religious. And no one was a more enthusiastic supporter than the late Carl Sagan. For him, SETI was not just a scientific project; it would be, quite literally, the source of the world's redemption. His reasoning went like this: Any society capable of transmitting messages to us must be far more technologically sophisticated than our own. Therefore, the receipt of a message from space would give us "an invaluable piece of knowledge," telling us "that it is possible to live through [the] technological adolescence" through which we are now passing.[15]

No such message has ever been detected, of course, yet Sagan offered detailed descriptions of the wondrous secrets we might learn if we ever succeed in decoding one. "It is possible," he exclaimed, "that among the first contents of such a message may be detailed prescriptions for the avoidance of technological disaster, for a passage through adolescence to maturity." Sagan never explained how an alien race that has never had any contact with Earth, a race whose chemistry and brains and language would be completely different from ours, would just happen to know exactly what our problems are, or how they would be capable of giving "detailed prescriptions" for solving them. Still, he seemed certain that they would offer advice for "straightforward solutions, still undiscovered on Earth, to problems of food shortages, population growth, energy supplies, dwindling resources, pollution, and war."[16]

Though disguised as science, this is nothing more than a magical vision of heavenly extraterrestrials emerging from the unknown to lift us from our misery. A longtime critic of SETI puts the matter bluntly: "It's a dream based on faith—a technological search for God."[17]

So this is where the great promise of science and technology leads us—not to a glorious earthly utopia, but to a fantasy-world escape from this planet and from the horrors that this same technology has created. This view of salvation is no more rational than the demented dreams of the Heaven's Gate cult—thirty-nine intelligent, well-educated people who ingested cocktails of alcohol and drugs in the hope that, by leaving their bodies behind, their spirits would meet up with a comet and move on to the "Level Above Human." In their case, the Escalator Myth proved deadly.

None of this scientific optimism, one should note, involves a change of heart. It is assumed that humanity's problems are not caused by wrong moral choices but by lack of knowledge. For example, Sagan promises that the longed-for message from outer space will teach us "the laws of development of civilizations" that will enable us to control society, just as knowing the laws of physics and chemistry enables us to control nature. What need is there for an awkward and troublesome thing like morality when we can control society for its own good through inviolable laws of "cultural evolution"?[18]

Yet history offers no evidence that knowledge alone will save human society. To the contrary, the problem with the Hitlers and Stalins of the world was not that they were stupid or ignorant of the laws of cultural evolution; the problem was that they were evil. Bigger and better technology simply gives people bigger and better means to carry out either good or evil choices.

PROPERLY UNDERSTOOD . . .

Having confidence in technology is a misguided form of salvation; some things are simply not amenable to a technical quick fix. It is the human heart that determines how we will use our machines—whether we will fashion them into swords or plowshares. Instead of scanning the skies for messages from other galaxies, it is far more realistic to seek the God who *made* those heavens and who came to reveal the truth by living among us. We don't need radio messages from extraterrestrials; we already have a message from God himself, and it is found in an ancient book that proclaimed the creation of the cosmos long before there were astronomers around to muse over such questions. The message begins: "In the beginning God created the heavens and the earth" (Gen. 1:1).

Properly understood, science is a wonderful tool for investigating God's world. But science cannot solve the human dilemma, and it cannot give us hope and meaning. And ultimately, those who exalt science into a religion discover this—which is why they finally give in to a profound pessimism, adrift on a space station called Earth, waiting for a beacon from beyond to save us from ourselves.

But for those less inclined to fantasy, there is no escape from the dreadful realization that a world without God can end only in despair.

CHAPTER 13

THE DRAMA OF DESPAIR

As you read, keep the following questions in mind:
- What is existentialism, and when, where, and why did it arise?
- How has a courage of despair redefined *courage*?
- What is sociobiology, and how has it moved far beyond true science?
- How does sociobiology express a philosophy of despair?

"The more the universe seems comprehensible, the more it also seems pointless." With these startling words, Nobel prize–winning physicist Steven Weinberg concludes *The First Three Minutes,* his book about the origin of the universe.[1]

Science reveals that we live in an "overwhelmingly hostile universe," Weinberg explains. It existed long before human beings appeared, and it is not going to remain habitable forever. According to current predictions, the universe is headed for a fiery death, and it will take us with it. Nothing we do will outlast our temporary span on this globe. Life is meaningless, purpose-less, "pointless."[2]

For many modern thinkers, the alternative to the Christian message of salvation is not any of the ersatz salvations we have discussed but a free fall into pessimism and despair. They have given up, deciding there *is* no transcendent purpose, no hope of redemption, no answer to life's most wrenching dilemmas, and the courageous person is the one who faces reality squarely and shakes off all illusory hopes. Yet, ironically, even this pessimism is often held with a fervor that resembles faith. Like the literary antihero, who is really the hero, this is an antifaith that actually functions as a faith.

EXISTENTIALISM AND THE END OF OPTIMISM

What happened to the utopian dreams of the past two centuries, the vision of endless upward progress? For many people, those dreams crashed in the convulsions of two world wars that left a trail of horrors, from the blood-soaked trenches of Argonne to the ashes of Auschwitz. From 1918 to 1945, a little more than a quarter century, the world was shocked out of its complacent optimism by the inescapable reality of naked evil.

European intellectuals who experienced the madness firsthand, on their native soil, were the first to preach a philosophy of despair. "There are no divine judges or controllers," proclaimed French philosopher Jean-Paul Sartre. "The world is all there is, our existence is all we have." Thus was born the word *existentialism*. In Sartre's play *No Exit*, one character distills the existentialist creed to a catch phrase: "You are your life, and that's all you are."[3] There is no higher purpose or goal or meaning to life.

Albert Camus, another post–World War II existentialist, probed the problem of meaninglessness in *The Myth of Sisyphus*, based on a story from classical mythology in which Sisyphus is punished by the gods who require him to push a boulder to the top of a hill, only to have it roll down again. For Camus, this mythological figure represents "the absurd hero," the person who recognizes the absurdity of existence and rebels against it. Since the universe is "without a master," Camus writes, all that's left for the absurd hero is to exercise his free choice and rebel, thereby becoming his own master.[4]

In the 1960s, the works of Sartre and Camus became wildly popular among American intellectuals and university students, feeding into the antiestablishment mood of the Vietnam era. If naturalistic science leads to the conclusion that there is no ultimate meaning to life—that life is absurd—then why not seek alternative sources of meaning in sensual pleasure and mind-altering drug experiences?

Make no mistake. The sixties was not just an era of long hair and bell-bottoms. It was an intellectual and cultural upheaval that marked the end of modernity's optimism and introduced the worldview of despair on a broad level. Ideas concocted in the rarefied domain of academia filtered down to shape an entire generation of young people. They, in turn, have brought those ideas to their logical conclusion in postmodernism, with its suspicion of the very notions of reason and objective truth.

HOSTILE TERRITORY

Of course, modernity has always had its dark underside. Already in the nineteenth century, sensitive people realized that science seemed to suggest an image of the universe that was hostile to human values. The world discovered by science was supposedly a world of mathematical entities: mass, extension, and velocity. The things that matter most to humans—purpose, meaning, love, and beauty— were relegated to the subjective realm of the mind, while human beings were reduced to an insignificant presence in an unthinking, unfeeling, purposeless world of masses spinning blindly in space. Science teaches us that mankind is no longer "the Heaven-descended heir of all the ages," said British philosopher Lord Balfour. "His very existence is an accident, his story a brief and transitory episode in the life of one of the meanest of the planets."[5]

It is a gloomy picture, but many people have found it all the more attractive for its gloom, shuddering "in delicious horror" before it, writes historian John Herman Randall. In fact, starting in the nineteenth century, "many believed it *because* it was so dreadful; they prided themselves on their courage in facing facts."[6]

A widely quoted example is from British philosopher Bertrand Russell's *A Free Man's Worship*. (With a title like that, Russell clearly understood that he was proposing an alternative faith). "Man is the product of causes which had no prevision of the end they were achieving; . . . his origin, his growth, his hopes and fears, his loves and his beliefs are but the outcome of accidental collocations of atoms." And finally, these proud, despairing words: "Only within the scaffolding of these truths, only on the firm foundation of unyielding despair, can the soul's habitation hence-forth be safely built."[7] One almost pictures Russell standing on a craggy rock, bloody but unbowed, his chin raised to the imper-sonal skies, proclaiming his credo to the uncaring elements.

A more recent example is the work of Nobel prize–winning biochemist Jacques Monod. In his celebrated *Chance and Necessity*, Monod rejects the Christian faith and replaces it with the drama of the scientist as lonely hero, challenging an alien and meaning-less universe. "Man must at last wake out of his millenary dream and discover his total solitude, his fundamental isolation. He must realize that, like a gypsy, he lives on the boundary of an alien world; a world that is deaf to his music, and as indifferent to his hopes as it is to his sufferings or his crimes."[8] This melodramatic portrait goes far beyond anything that could properly be called science. It clearly expresses a faith, or, more accurately, an anti-faith: The world is hostile to all that makes us human, yet we will overcome our cosmic loneliness through heroic defiance.

The creeds of pessimism often take on a distinctly Darwinist cast. Darwin's theory suggests that human beings are merely advanced animals competing in the struggle for existence—that nature is "red in tooth and claw," in the words of Alfred, Lord Tennyson. All life-forms are driven to compete for the next rung on the evolutionary ladder, leaving the weak behind. In the late nineteenth and early twentieth centuries, these ideas were enshrined in social Darwinism—the idea that the rich and corrupt are in power because they've proven themselves the "fittest" in the struggle for survival and that there's nothing we can do about it because it's simply the law of nature. Moral persuasion and spiritual redemption are irrelevant because we are trapped in an endless struggle to reach the top of the heap.

GENE MACHINES

This dark side of Darwinism remained an undercurrent, causing few ripples in the reigning myth of progress until recent decades, when it burst forth in what is known as *sociobiology*—today often called evolutionary psychology. Sociobiology is an attempt to explain what evolution implies for human values. In doing so, it tends to take on the functions of religion, for it is impossible to discuss values without stumbling onto the most basic religious questions.

Starting with the Darwinian assumption that those who are most competitive come out on top, sociobiologists conclude that evolution requires ruthlessly selfish behavior. Even actions that appear to be aimed at the benefit of others are grounded in underlying selfishness: We are nice to others only so they will be nice to us. Love and altruism are illusions, cover-ups for underlying self-interest. In the words of one sociobiologist, there is "no hint of genuine charity" among humans or any other organism. Though an organism may sometimes find himself forced to act in ways that benefit others, still, "given a full chance to act in his own interest, nothing but expediency will restrain him from brutalizing, from maiming, from murdering—his brother, his mate, his parent, or his child."[9] In the cold light of science, we turn out to be selfish to the core.

What a ferocious picture of life—and taken at face value, it is a rather ridiculous one. No human society exists without altruism, charity, and cooperation. Yet these can be explained away, insists the sociobiologist. According to the theory, the real agents of evolution are the genes, and their only interest is in surviving and being passed on to the next generation. Even when we are engaged in apparently altruistic behavior, we are actually being duped by our genes, which are busily stacking the deck in their favor. Thus, the mother sacrifices selflessly for her child, but she does so only because her genes compel her to take care of the child, who is the vehicle for her genes to survive into the future.

Now, we might agree that taking care of our own family members has a tinge of self-interest. But what about cooperation and altruism that reach beyond family and kin? What about the heroic passerby who rescues a drowning child? Even that is reducible to genetic selfishness, says science writer Mark Ridley in *The Origins of Virtue*. He argues that any organism intelligent enough to remember individuals and keep tabs will discover that it is sometimes in our interest to help others—because they might someday help us in return. And if it's in our interest, then it will be preserved by natural selection. Even the most selfless behavior can be explained by selfish genes.[10]

Far beyond Science

But notice how the claims of sociobiology have moved far beyond science and into the realm of myth, where the gene is personified as the hero of the plot. In Ridley's account, for example, the genes weigh the pros and cons of cooperative behavior and "program" us accordingly, as if genes had the logical capacity of a computer expert.[11] British science writer Richard Dawkins insists that humans are nothing more than "machines created by our genes," as if genes were engineers capable of designing and building complex mechanisms.[12] Or consider a famous line from Edward O. Wilson, the founder of sociobiology: "The organism is only DNA's way of making more DNA," as if genes were capable of planning and making things. Wilson even argues that the ultimate source of human morality is the "morality of the gene," making genes capable of moral reasoning and choice.[13]

In short, sociobiology attributes consciousness, will, and choice to genes, while reducing humans to machines that carry out their orders. This is a worldview in which genes become the deity—the ultimate creators and controllers of life.

Of course, when pressed, sociobiologists will say this is all metaphorical, not intended to be taken literally. And yet, a consistent and pervasive metaphor eventually shapes the way we think. Even scientists themselves go back and forth, speaking sometimes as if they take the idea of selfish genes literally. "I shall argue that a predominant quality to be expected in a successful gene is ruthless selfishness," writes Dawkins. "Let us try to teach generosity and altruism, because we are born selfish."[14] Notice how he leaps from genes to humans, using the word "selfish" in exactly the same sense, with all its moral connotations. In the "religion of the gene," selfishness is the original sin.

"Like successful Chicago gangsters," Dawkins goes on, spinning his colorful tale, "our genes have survived, in some cases for millions of years, in a highly competitive world," and preserving our genes is "the *ultimate rationale* for our existence." Dawkins argues, "By dictating the way survival machines [that's us] and their nervous systems are built, genes exert *ultimate power* over behavior." Finally, Dawkins waxes positively lyrical. The gene "does not grow old. It leaps from body to body down the generations, manipulating body after body in its own way and for its own ends, abandoning a succession of mortal bodies before they sink in senility and death. The genes are the immortals."[15]

The immortals? Dawkins offers this as sober science, but to speak about an immortal force with "ultimate power" over our lives, giving us the "ultimate rationale" for living, is clearly a religious statement.

Indeed, sociobiology has all the essential elements of religion. It tells us where we came from: Random chemicals linked up to form the rudimentary DNA, until finally some DNA discovered how to construct bodies for themselves. It tells us what's wrong with us: The fatal flaw in human nature is that we are selfish— a selfishness that reaches far beyond our conscious moral choices and is firmly embedded in our genes. But whereas most worldviews go on to offer a proposal for remedying the basic flaw in human nature, sociobiology offers no remedy. It presents the human being as a puppet in the control of immoral, scheming genes, with no real hope of ever breaking free. It is a religion with no hope of redemption. Life is reduced to perpetual warfare, while the gene is transformed into an evil and destructive demon, driven to overcome all competitors in the struggle for existence.

Thus, sociobiology can be understood as a contemporary form of those fatalistic religions that tap into the human fascination with power, death, and destruction. After all, the Greeks and Romans worshiped the gods of death (Pluto) and war (Mars). The Babylonians worshiped Nergal, a god of death and pestilence. The Hindu god Siva and his wife, Kali, stand for death and destruction. Similarly, in sociobiology the "deity being worshipped is power," writes British philosopher Mary Midgley. Adherents "offer us a mystique of power" located in the genes.[16]

What could possibly be appealing about such a negative faith? Despite its pessimism, it offers one compensation: It gives adherents a way to debunk conventional religion and morality. It dispels the "illusion" that there is a loving, sovereign God and that human beings have dignity and significance as genuine moral agents.

If you wonder whether we are reading too much into

sociobiology, just dip into the writings of Edward O. Wilson, founder of the movement. Wilson admits that he left his Baptist tradition at the age of fifteen and transferred his religious longings elsewhere: "My heart continued to believe in the light and the way . . . and I looked for grace in some other setting"—which turned out to be science. Having entered "the temple of science," Wilson shifted his faith to the "mythology" of scientific materialism, and then searched for a "single grand naturalistic image of man" that would explain everything "as a material process, from the bottom up, atoms to genes to the human spirit."[17]

Wilson is completely candid that his goal is to "divert the power of religion" into the service of materialism or naturalism. "Make no mistake about the power of scientific materialism," he warns. It is a philosophy that presents "an alternative mythology" that has repeatedly "defeated traditional religion."[18]

Reality Test

But has it, in fact, defeated traditional religion? Not at all, for sociobiology or evolutionary psychology itself fails a basic test of any truth claim: It is not an accurate portrayal of either human nature or human society. Common experience and common sense—bolstered by the findings of sociology and anthropology—easily debunk its excessively dark picture of unmitigated competition and slavery to the power of selfish genes.

It is seriously misleading to apply the word *selfish* to an object that has no self—namely, the gene. When we talk about changes in gene frequencies, that's science. But if we say that humans are helpless puppets whose strings are in the hands of calculating genes, that's mythology. When we say that humans are influenced by their genes, that's science. But if we say that genes are "selfish"—that they are "hidden masters" who have "programmed" us to "serve" them—that's mythology.

Science does not compel us to adopt sociobiology or any other pessimistic worldview that denies the reality of redemption and dramatizes nature as a stage for perpetual conflict. Indeed, many pessimists engage in circular reasoning: First they banish God and conclude that the universe is meaningless; then they argue that since the universe is meaningless, there cannot be a God. Atheism is presented as the *conclusion* when it is, in fact, the hidden *premise.*

And if your premise is rejection of the biblical God, then no matter how sophisticated your theories, they will end in despair. For these pessimistic myths are right about one thing: A universe without God is indeed impersonal, meaningless, and purposeless. It is, to echo Weinberg, pointless.

DEFYING DEATH

A full-page ad for Schwinn bicycles shows a young man leaping high into the air on his Schwinn; at the bottom of the page is a picture of a coffin being lowered into the ground. The ad copy taunts the reader: "What, a little death frightens you?" Schwinn is clearly marketing more than bikes; it is telling kids that it is cool to court death.

Since when did playing with death become chic? Since a pervasive sense of meaninglessness has left many people so jaded that it takes more than a whiff of danger to restore a sense of ultimacy. And what is more intense, more ultimate, than coming face-to-face with death?

This mind-set may explain the growing popularity of high-risk sports, from hang gliding to rock climbing, from street luge to skydiving. When *U.S. News and World Report* ran a cover story on the topic of high-risk sports, one subhead read: "The peril, the thrill, the sheer rebellion of it all."[19] Like Camus's absurd hero, this is rebellion against the absurdity, against the futility of life, where everything we love or live for ends in death. In a society reduced to sterile secularism, the only response left is to look death squarely in the face . . . and spit on it. This is the ultimate, heroic existentialist response.

Kristen Ulmer, an icon of the "extreme sports" crowd, says she took up "extreme skiing" (maneuvers that deliberately expose one to danger) to combat boredom. She insists she gets a thrill from any kind of risk or danger, and she suggests spicing up conventional sports by injecting more danger: "It's one thing to be a really good basketball player. But imagine if every time you missed a basket, somebody would shoot you in the head. It would be a lot more exciting, right?"[20]

In the Midwest, several companies offer to take tourists out to chase tornadoes. What's the attraction? The excitement of a brush with death. One man told NBC news that coming close to a tornado was "a religious experience."[21] This is all that's left for a culture that has plumbed the depths of absurdity: daredevil antics in the face of death.

And when the antics grow old, there is only death itself. Ernest Hemingway, one of this century's great novelists, held to the existentialist credo that life is "a short day's journey from nothingness to nothingness."[22] To give meaning to that nothingness, Hemingway invented his own code: He would taste life to the fullest— experience everything, feel everything, do everything. Even death could be overcome if he treated it as another experience, the most exciting and interesting experience of all.

And so, at age sixty-one, after a life of notoriety as a big-game hunter, adventurer, and womanizer, Hemingway deliberately embraced death. He could no longer prove that he was master of his own fate by his daredevil adventures or self-indulgent lifestyle, but he could prove it by controlling the time and means of his own death.

On Sunday morning, July 2, 1961, Hemingway loaded his favorite gun, seated himself in the foyer of his Idaho home, braced the butt of the gun on the floor, put the barrel in his mouth, and pulled the trigger.

Neurotic? Sick? Perhaps not. Given his worldview, Hemingway's action was eminently logical. After all, if life is meaningless and despair crouches like a lion at the gate, the best option might be to exit heroically on your own terms. Ernest Hemingway shook his fist at despair one last time by taking control of his own death.[23]

IN THE END

In the end, those who deny the God of the Bible and of history, and who find the myth of progress empty, have only two choices: They can either trivialize death by defying it or control death by embracing it on their own terms. Thus, Hemingway is the perfect icon for the failure of Western science and philosophy: Having played out the logical consequences of the Enlightenment's rejection of God, many people are brought to complete despair of any transcendent truth or meaning. The blazing, optimistic hope that humanity is moving ever upward and onward, boldly progressing to a new stage in evolution, has been replaced by bitter cynicism. Marooned on the rocks of reality, science itself now promises only the near comical fantasy that humanity might be rescued by extraterrestrials from outer space.

One might think that upon hitting the dead end of despair, men and women would be driven to return to the Creator. But, alas, although it is true that "our hearts find no peace until they rest in [God]," the basic human instinct is to flee him.[24] For finding God will cost us our cherished autonomy.

So where do many people turn? To the East.

DISCUSSION QUESTIONS

CHAPTER 11

1 What biblical parallels of redemption can you see in Sanger's philosophy of sexuality?

2 Paraphrase and list some of the false assumptions identified in the text of this chapter. Examples: Self-denial is a "cruel morality." All orgasms are morally the same. Select two or three of these premises and discuss how you would counter them in conversation with a young person who has accepted them as "gospel truth." (Note: Spend some time on this question, which is a different version of the role play activity of previous sessions.)

CHAPTER 12

3 Summarize the myth of science as savior. What has become the substitute for Christian hope?

4 Why is science unable to give any moral guidance?

5 Without moral guidelines, what dangers are inherent in the scientific version of the Escalator Myth?

6 What unrealistic expectation is at the heart of the Escalator Myth? What are the ramifications of this expectation? What basic Christian truth(s) provide(s) a critical reality check absent in this myth?

7 Where does the great promise of science and technology lead us? To use the words of Alice in Wonderland, why does this seem "curiouser and curiouser"?

8 Read aloud Genesis 11:1-9, the story of a primitive society with lofty ideals and high hopes. Brainstorm a list of adjectives that describe these people.

9 To what did these people aspire? Paraphrase those hopes and dreams in a way that also describes goals of contemporary secular worldviews.

10 How did God view this project? How did he respond?

11 Here God used a simple cultural artifact—language—to thwart the people's errant plans. What does this tell you about God's creativity in his dealings with mankind? In what creative ways can you counter the arrogance (refer also to the other adjectives you listed in question 12) of people whose goals run contrary to a Christian worldview? (Think again of influences that drew Dr. Bernard Nathanson to the Christian faith.)

CHAPTER 13

12 For someone who views the world as being essentially hostile to humanity, what is the basis for courage and heroism?

13 It's all in your genes, and "their only interest is in surviving and being passed on to the next generation." From your personal experience does it seem that all altruism is reducible to genetic selfishness? Give examples and draw conclusions based on logic.

14 In what ways has sociobiology turned science to myth?

15 If one sees that the various utopian dreams are indeed mythic and unrealizable, and if one doesn't believe in God, how can courage (a classical virtue) become antithetical to virtue? What does this mean for you as parents? How can you encourage

people, especially young people, to have courage with good
purpose and for right reasons?

16 "If we *can* do it, we should." Whether the issue is sex or
science or suicide, what aspects of a biblical worldview prompt
you to say, "Not so fast. Let's look at the issues here . . ." ?

CLOSING SUMMARY

What is the one thing you want to remember from what you read
(or heard or did) in this session?

Consider sharing this with the group.

NEW AGE OR REAL
REDEMPTION?

*Men and women have ultimately
come up from amoebas, [and] they
are ultimately on their way
towards God.*   KEN WILBER

CHAPTER 1 4

THAT NEW AGE RELIGION

As you read, keep the following questions in mind:
- In what way is the New Age movement different from the classic Eastern religions?
- What are the basic New Age beliefs, and how do they differ from Christianity?
- What temptation is at the heart of New Age thinking?

When the bright image of science and progress began to fade, and optimism gave way to disillusionment and despair, many people began to cast about for answers from other cultures. Asian religions, especially Hinduism and Buddhism, have always enchanted people from Western cultures to some degree, and today these religions have become popular alternatives to the dominant Western worldview.

POWERFUL ATTRACTION

And the attraction is powerful. Western secularism is materialistic, limiting reality to what can be tested scientifically. Eastern mysticism is spiritual, opening the consciousness to new levels of awareness. Western thought is analytical, leading to fragmentation and alienation. Eastern thought is holistic, promising healing and wholeness. Western science has destroyed the environment and polluted the air. Eastern pantheism proffers a new respect for nature.

In the 1960s, many young people turned to Eastern religion to fill their spiritual emptiness, giving rise to the New Age movement. Today the movement has become so mainstream that community colleges offer classes in yoga, tai chi, astrology, and therapeutic touch. The New Age movement is also a major commercial success. Local supermarkets carry free copies of slick New Age publications, advertising everything from holistic health practices to past-life therapy.

Buddhism swept the silver screen with *Kundun* (which is Tibetan for "the presence") and *Seven Years in Tibet*. In the latter, Brad Pitt donned a white sari and shaved his head for his role as Heinrich Harrer, an Austrian who escapes from a World War II British prison in India and reaches Lhasa, where he comes under the influence of the young Dalai Lama. Pitt reportedly asked for the role because he wanted the religious experience. After each day's shooting, Buddhist monks would pray for the set and invite the cast to sing with them. Pitt was often in tears.[1]

Actor Richard Gere is even more devout. In 1984, he converted to Tibetan Buddhism and now spends several months each year traveling and speaking on behalf of the Dalai Lama. Then there is Steven Segal, who has been recognized by the supreme head of the Tibetan-based Nyingma lineage as a *tulku* (a reincarnated lama), as well as a *terton* (a revealer of truth). Think of that the next time you watch Segal on film breaking an enemy's neck.[2]

It's not difficult to see why Eastern religion is such an attractive form of salvation for a post-Christian culture. It assuages the ego by pronouncing the individual divine, and it gives a gratifying sense of "spirituality" without making any demands in terms of doctrinal commitment or ethical living. And to make it even more palatable, the New Age movement reshapes Eastern thought to fit the Western mind, with its hunger for upward progress.

Whereas Eastern thinking is fatalistic and pessimistic—the cycle of karma is called the "wheel of suffering"—<u>the New Age adaptation is optimistic and utopian. It promises that if we get in touch with the "Universal Spirit," of which we are all part, we will create a new consciousness and a new world.</u> The New Age movement is premised on the promise that we are on the threshold of a great leap forward into, literally, a new age—of "harmony and understanding, sympathy and trust abounding," to quote the musical *Hair.*[3] The massive social upheavals of the past decades are not a warning of imminent disaster but the prelude to evolutionary transformation. As New Age writer Ken Wilber puts it, "Men and women have ultimately come up from amoebas, [and] they are ultimately on their way towards God."[4] Toward *becoming* God, Wilber means. Humanity, he suggests, is about to make a quantum leap forward, to emerge as an entirely new creature, to become divine. This is nothing but the Escalator Myth in spiritualized form.

ROMANTIC ORIGINS OF SPIRITUAL EVOLUTION

It may seem that the New Age movement appeared out of nowhere in the 1960s, but the way had been prepared by the nineteenth-century romantic movement, which was a kind of counterculture in its own day. As we saw in the last chapter, back then sensitive people could already see that science was creating a picture of the world as a vast machine, inexorably grinding its gears, with no place for beauty or meaning or purpose. The romantics cast about for an alternative, just as the children of the sixties did, and they revived an ancient philosophy known as neo-Platonism, a blend of Greek thought and Eastern mysticism. They tossed out the metaphor of the universe as a machine and replaced it with the metaphor of the universe as an organism, a living thing, animated by a "Life Force."

Everything is alive, the romantics said. Even matter itself, they thought, has a rudimentary form of life or consciousness. And what is the major characteristic of life? Growth. Development. The romantics proposed that just as each organism unfolds in stages according to an inner law of development, so life itself unfolds in definite stages from simple to complex under the direction of the Life Force. The Life Force often took on the trappings of an immanent deity, so that God was conceived not as the transcendent creator, but as a spirit pervading nature. "The world was no machine, it was alive," writes historian John Herman Randall, "and God was not its creator so much as its soul, its life."[5]

The publication of Darwin's *Origin of Species* gave the concept of spiritual evolution a big boost. Most people who accepted Darwinian evolution were not atheists; instead, they tried to integrate it in some way with religion by identifying God with a force that gives purpose and direction to evolution. But the end result was often more akin to pantheism than to orthodox Christianity. This God was completely immanent in the world, compelling evolution to ever greater heights and leading mankind to some far-off divine perfection. As Alfred, Lord Tennyson wrote, there is "One God, one law, one element, / And one far-off divine event, / To which the whole creation moves."[6]

Spiritual evolution often reduced God to a participant in the process, a "God-in-the-making," who was gradually evolving along with the world into full divinity. In the early twentieth century, philosopher Henri Bergson reduced God to a vital force animating all life and driving evolution forward. The great philosopher Alfred North Whitehead pictured God as the soul of the world, changing as the world changes, striving toward perfection. And the role of humans is to help God actualize himself. As theologian Charles Hartshorne puts it, we are "co-creators" with God, not only in making the world but also in making God himself.[7] We have met some of these ideas before in chapter 7 under the label of process theology, the fastest-growing theology in America today.

What we see is that for a long time, in philosophy, the arts, and even theology, the Western world has been embracing ideas compatible with Eastern pantheism. All it took was a widespread disillusionment with Western culture to send these ideas hurtling into the mainstream.

NEW AGE IN THE CLASSROOM

Today, New Age thinking permeates Western society, spawning a host of techniques used in medicine, business, education, the military, and even—tragically—churches. Various meditation exercises are sold as means for resolving conflict and for enhancing relaxation, creativity, self-esteem, and even physical health. For example, at Stanford University's Graduate School of Business, a seminar listed as Creativity in Business includes meditation, chanting, "dream work," tarot cards, and a discussion of "the New Age Capitalist."[8] Government agencies as well as private businesses spend millions of dollars in contracts with consulting companies that use New Age techniques for management training.[9]

Of course, these programs rarely use overtly religious language. For example, the Universal Spirit (Brahma, in classic Hindu thought) is often called the Higher Self or some similar term. Yet beneath the secular rhetoric, these programs embody the basic Hindu doctrine that the individual human mind or spirit is part of a Universal Mind or Spirit, and that by using relaxation and guided imagery exercises, we can tap into that Mind as a source of wisdom and creativity.[10]

New Age programs have even permeated our elementary and secondary schools. A mother in Atlanta, Georgia, was concerned when her second-grade daughter failed to respond to her one day when they were driving in the car. The mother called the girl's

name repeatedly and finally turned around to look in the backseat.
Her daughter's eyes were closed and her head drooped forward.
Alarmed, the woman stopped the car, opened the back door, and
shook her daughter's arm. The girl jerked awake, as if startled out
of a trance.

"What's wrong?" the mother asked anxiously. "You wouldn't
answer when I called."

"Don't worry, Mom," the little girl replied. "I was with my
friend Pumsy."

Questioning her daughter further, the mother discovered that
the girl had been learning meditation techniques from the school's
guidance counselor through a curriculum titled *PUMSY in Pursuit
of Excellence.* Pumsy is a cute, fairy-tale dragon who discovers a
wise guide named Friend, who teaches Pumsy (along with the
children in the program) basic concepts of the Eastern worldview.
For example, Friend tells Pumsy that her mind is like a pool of
water: When she is tempted to think negative thoughts, her mind
is muddy. But when she thinks positive thoughts, she can tap into
a Clear Mind, which will help her solve her problems.[11]

There's a reason the term *Clear Mind* is capitalized: It's another
cover-up term for Brahma, the god of Hinduism. One clue is the
quasi-religious language used to describe it. For example, Friend
tells Pumsy, "Your Clear Mind is the best friend you'll ever
have. . . . It is always close to you, and it will never leave you."
This sounds suspiciously close to biblical language: "I will never
leave you nor forsake you" (Josh. 1:5). A few pages later in the
story, we read, "You have to trust [your Clear Mind] and let it
do good things for you."[12] Through this program, children are
essentially being taught to place religious trust in a Hindu notion
of God as a Universal Mind.

Of course, such New Age techniques are not sold to teachers
as religion. They are marketed as ways to increase creativity and
boost self-esteem. PUMSY teaches youngsters to chant slogans

like "I can handle it," "I can make it happen," and "I am me, I am enough." Once again, we hear echoes of biblical themes: "I am who I am" (Exod. 3:14). This program is teaching self-worship, not self-esteem. <u>It's teaching that we are saved not by trusting a transcendent God who reaches down to us in grace but by realizing that God is within us, that *we* are God.</u> Salvation is not a matter of recognizing our sin; it's a matter of raising our consciousness until we recognize our inner divinity.[13]

NEW AGE ON THE BOOKSHELVES

Education is only one avenue for New Age ideas. They turn up in every outlet of popular culture. Books about the New Age, for example, enjoy a commanding position on bookstore shelves, often crowding out traditional religious works. If you opened a book and read, "I looked and saw a new heaven and a new earth," you might think you were reading the book of Revelation in the Bible. Instead, it is the opening of James Redfield's megahit *The Tenth Insight.* The words are indeed from Revelation, but that's the closest link to anything biblical. As the story unfolds, the author weaves his own New Age philosophy into the plot. We learn that, before birth, we are all part of a great spiritual force pervading the universe. We can reconnect to this force—or "achieve union with God"—by recalling what it was like to be part of God before we were born. That knowledge is recaptured by tuning into the "spirit within"—to the fragment of the Universal Spirit that remains in all of us. If enough people make this connection, Redfield claims, society will be transformed. Evil and crime will disappear; poverty and disease will be wiped out. We will live in perfect harmony—just as pictured in the book of Revelation.[14]

Even Christians can be disarmed by the subtleties of the New Age. "You must read this book," an enthusiastic friend told

Nancy, handing her a copy of *The Secret Garden* by Frances Hodgson Burnett, first published in 1911. The friend was a thoughtful Christian mother, and the book is a children's classic. But Nancy was jolted when she discovered that the book is Hindu philosophy dressed up in a charming children's story.

In the words of ten-year-old Colin, one of the book's main characters, the world is made of a single spiritual substance, which he calls Magic (always capitalized). "Everything is made out of Magic, leaves and trees, flowers and birds, badgers and foxes and squirrels and people," says Colin.[15] "The Magic is in me. . . . It's in every one of us."[16] This is classic pantheism, and Burnett entwines it with language right out of the Christian creeds. "Magic is always . . . making things out of nothing," says Colin.[17]

The difference between this pantheistic deity and the biblical God is that this is an impersonal force that can be tapped, like an electric current. As Colin says, we need to learn how to "get hold of it [Magic] and make it do things for us—like electricity and horses and steam."[18] This is not a Lord to be obeyed but a force to be manipulated. And the way to do that is through spells and incantations. Thus, Colin chants, "The Magic is in me. . . . Magic! Magic! Come and help!"[19]

Ironically, a few years after Nancy read *The Secret Garden* and dissected its New Age themes, her son was assigned the book to read—in a Christian school. We must be on guard to know what our children are reading in school.

THE PRIMAL TEMPTATION

Clearly, the New Age movement should not be laughed off as a silly fad. It is the vehicle for disseminating a complete worldview, offering an answer to all three major life questions. *Where did we come from, and who are we?* We are somehow fragmented off from the Universal Spirit. *What has gone wrong with the world?* We have forgotten our true nature, forgotten that we are part of God. *What is the source of our salvation?* We must rediscover our true nature and link up to the God within.

Like all forms of the Escalator Myth, this one starts with utopian premises. There is no real evil, only ignorance: We have forgotten who we are. And by the same token, there is no real redemption, only enlightenment: We must recover a mystical knowledge of our inner divinity. This we do by various techniques, such as meditation, relaxation exercises, guided imagery, visualization, and use of crystals—all aimed at producing a state of consciousness in which the boundaries of the self dissolve and we gain a sense of unity with the divine. Through this higher consciousness, a person is said to tap into divine power and become more creative, more energetic, and even capable of healing illnesses through the power of the mind.

But like all forms of utopianism, this offer of salvation is hollow. By denying the reality of sin, it fails to address the crucial truth of our existence—that we are fallen creatures prone to evil. Proponents of the New Age reassure us that alienation and strife exist only on the superficial level of existence; at the deepest level, we are one with each other in God. As we become aware of this unity, they assert, we will begin to treat each other with kindness and charity.

However, this view of human nature simply doesn't stack up against reality. Mere knowledge is not enough to undercut the evil in the human heart. Simply *knowing* what is right doesn't enable us to *do* right. This is the dilemma the apostle Paul wrestled with: The good that I want to do, I don't do (see especially Rom. 7:14-25). We don't need to raise our consciousness; we need to be saved.

The New Age deity cannot save us. It is an impersonal spiritual substratum of energy underlying all things. He—or rather, it—is more akin to electricity than to a deity. It is a power people try to plug into, not a personal God they can love and communicate with.

Moreover, for all its promises about raising self-esteem, the New Age gospel does nothing to affirm the worth of the individual; it offers no basis for human dignity and meaning. On the contrary, the goal of all meditation techniques is to lose the individual self, to dissolve it in the Universal Spirit, just as a drop of water dissolves in the ocean. How utterly unlike the biblical God, who created us as individuals, who watches over each of us and numbers "even the very hairs of [our] head" (Matt. 10:30).

Furthermore, New Age philosophy gives us no basis for morality. If God is in everything, God is in both good and evil; therefore, there is no final difference between them. Morality is reduced to a method for purifying the soul from desires so that it can attain mystical consciousness, like the eightfold path of Buddhism.[20]

But the ultimate failure of New Age thinking is its sheer implausibility. How many of us are capable of insisting, with a straight face, that we are perfect? Yet New Age proponents actually claim that "we are perfect exactly the way we are. And when we accept that, life works."[21] People who can swallow that have to be deliberately oblivious to their own failures, shortcomings, and sins.

And how many of us are capable of claiming, without sounding as if we've escaped from an asylum, that we are God, the ultimate reality, the absolute spirit? In a scene in Shirley MacLaine's television miniseries *Out on a Limb,* the star shows how she had to be coached by her New Age counselor to shout "I am God" over and over until she could say it with confidence.[22] It takes some doing to convince ourselves, against all the evidence, that we are divine. And those who succeed in doing so have simply given in to the oldest temptation in human history: the impulse to self-deification, humanity's primal temptation. "You will not surely die," the serpent promised. "You will be like God" (Gen. 3:4-5).

In short, spiritual evolutionism is not merely an error, a mistaken idea; it is religious rebellion against reality—against the sheer fact that God is the Creator and we are creatures. It is the empty boast of the pot that claims to make itself without the need of a Potter.

A GOD IN OUR OWN IMAGE

The pantheism that underlies New Age thought has appeared in so many periods of history and in so many guises that C. S. Lewis considered it the religion that we fall into naturally, apart from divine revelation: "the natural bent of the human mind . . . the attitude into which the human mind automatically falls when left to itself." Therefore, Lewis notes, pantheism is "the only really formidable opponent" to Christianity.[23]

And today it is making inroads even into Christian institutions. Mainstream churches hold "Re-Imagining" conferences denouncing the biblical God as patriarchal and holding worship services to "our mother, Sophia" (the Greek name for wisdom).[24] Christian apologist Peter Kreeft says that at Boston College, where he teaches, most students enter as pantheists: "Most of my Catholic college students believe we are parts of God and that God is in everyone." As a result, they don't believe we need to be saved; we "need only recognize our intrinsic value and accept ourselves as we are."[25] No wonder many people anticipate that the great confrontation of the next century will be between the New Age movement and orthodox Christianity (represented largely by evangelicalism, conservative Roman Catholicism, and the Orthodox church).

The danger is that as more and more Christians regard religion as therapy, we lower our defenses against worldviews that appeal primarily to our emotions while demanding nothing. The New Age is the perfect religious match for a culture driven by a therapeutic mind-set, hungry to fill the nothingness. It allows its followers to draw on ancient wisdom but to reshape it to fit the fashion of the moment.

By contrast, Christianity makes stringent moral demands on its followers. Critics often dismiss Christianity as mere wish fulfillment, a comforting illusion dreamed up by the ancients. But this characterization is patently foolish. Who, after all, would invent a religion that commands us to give up our lives for one another, to overcome evil with good, to love our enemies, to turn the other cheek, to give our possessions to the poor, to be just and merciful? Would anyone really design a religion devoted to an all-powerful, sovereign, omniscient God who demands righteousness and obedience? A God who dispenses severe judgment?

No. When people create their own religion, they create gods and goddesses in their own image. The ancient gods of mythology had limited powers, were subject to human interference, and displayed all the human weaknesses and vices. And the New Age god, who is little more than a warm feeling within or at worst a dabbling in occult powers, is merely a ratification of whatever the human ego wants.

In the final analysis, any religious worldview must pass the most crucial test: Can it make sense of the human predicament? Does it offer genuine redemption? Is it true? Applying this test to the New Age worldview, we detect its fatal weaknesses. It fails to correspond to reality as we experience it.

And if there is no answer in the West and no answer in the East, where does one turn?

CHAPTER 15

REAL REDEMPTION

As you read, keep the following questions in mind:
- What solution does Christianity provide to the problem of sin?
- On what historical basis is Christianity grounded?
- "Only Christianity provides true redemption?" What does this mean?

Modern pluralistic society provides a smorgasbord of world-views and belief systems, all clamoring for our allegiance. And whether their trappings are secular or religious, all are in essence offering means of salvation—attempts to solve the human dilemma and give hope for renewing the world. Today's most fashionable answers presume there is no kingdom of God on which to fasten our eschatological hopes, and therefore, they promise to create heaven here on earth—the Escalator Myth in its various forms. Alongside these are messages of heroic despair, challenging us to be courageous in facing life's meaninglessness.

It is easy to become bewildered by the array of answers available in today's marketplace of ideas, to throw up one's hands and declare them all valid options. That's why pluralism often leads to relativism—to the idea that there *is* no overarching, objective truth but only a variety of subjective beliefs. As

Catholic scholar Ronald Knox once quipped, "The study of comparative religions is the best way to become comparatively religious."[1] Sadly, that maxim often holds true.

Yet a careful examination of competing worldviews can actually lead to the opposite effect: By lining up the Christian faith against other worldviews and religions, as we have done in the previous chapters, we see with astonishing clarity that Christianity offers the only real answers to the most basic questions of life and the best understanding of how we can be saved.

ACCURATE DIAGNOSIS

First, Christianity begins with an accurate diagnosis of the human dilemma. The basic problem is a moral one: our guilt before a holy God. God created us and established the moral dimensions for our lives. But we blew it. We have sinned, every one of us; we all have fallen short of God's perfect standard (Rom. 3:23). We have defied the moral order of the universe, and as a result, we are alienated from God.

Admittedly, people often do not *feel* guilty before God, since we are indoctrinated with the belief that guilt is merely a subjective feeling, a neurosis to be cured, and that we really ought to feel good about ourselves. As a result, many people come to Christianity on grounds other than guilt: a longing for inner peace and purpose, an attraction to the quality of love practiced in a local church, or a need to resolve some life crisis. But no matter what initially attracts us to Christianity, at some point each of us must confront the truth of our own moral condition: Guilt is objectively real, and *we* are guilty. We are sinners in the hands of a righteous God. The Holy Spirit can penetrate the hardest heart to convict us of our sinfulness. I know, because that is exactly what the Spirit did in my life.

THE ONLY ANSWER

Second, <u>Christianity provides the only answer to the problem of sin.</u> God himself has reached across the moral chasm that separates us from him in order to bring us back. The second person of the Trinity became a human being, lived a perfect life of obedience to the moral order, and in his death paid the price for our violation of the moral law, satisfying the demands of divine justice. God's solution reveals a marvelous economy, for the substitutionary atonement permits God to be both "just and the one who justifies" (Rom. 3:26). He remains "just" because he does not merely turn a blind eye to humanity's violation of the moral law, which flows from his own holy character. Yet at the same time he "justifies" those who have violated that law because its demands have been met by Christ's suffering on the cross.

Since it is humans who commit sin, only a human being can pay the penalty for it. But since sin offends an infinite Being, the penalty is infinite—which means only God can pay it. Thus the Incarnation is the only reasonable and fitting solution: God becomes man in order, as man, to pay the penalty for our sin.

But death of the God-man is not the end of the story, for Jesus was resurrected from the dead and lives forever. He overcame death, making it possible for us to be free from sin and death, from evil and destruction. By accepting his salvation, we become new creations and a new people. This is the "good news" (the literal meaning of *gospel*) that Christianity offers. And it is far more than a mere intellectual answer; it transforms our lives. For myself, I know that I could not live with myself if I hadn't experienced the overwhelming conviction one night in 1973, sitting in my car in a friend's driveway, that God had died *for me*. In a flood of tears, I felt released from a crushing sense of guilt and revived with a new sense of purpose and meaning. For the first time, I had a real reason for living.

All the ideologies we've examined in this section are pallid imitations of the Christian gospel. They promise to free people from oppression (or neurosis, or whatever else they define as the problem) and create the New Man, build the New Society, usher in the New Age. Clinging to the beauty of the gospel's hope but wanting none of the gospel's requirements, they recast it as the Escalator Myth, a fallacy of progress, promising that we can create a new life through politics, sex, science, or Eastern spirituality. But all of these worldviews are defective, inadequate substitutes for the real need of real people for real redemption.

HISTORICAL TRUTH

Third, Christianity's offer of salvation is based on historical truth. The final element that sets Christianity apart from all other religions and worldviews is that it is based not on some evolutionary projection millions of years into the future or on some extraterrestrial fantasy, but on a historical event at a specific time and place: the crucifixion of Christ during the Jewish Passover in Jerusalem in the year A.D. 30 and his resurrection three days later.[2]

During the two thousand years since Christ's resurrection, the historical validity of this event has withstood every imaginable assault, ranging from the charge of "a cover-up" (by religious leaders of Jesus' day) to modern claims that it was a "Passover plot" or a "conjuring trick with bones." What skeptics overlook is that the empty tomb was a historical fact, verifiable by ordinary observation like any other historical fact. It was acknowledged by the soldiers who guarded the tomb (why else did they need to concoct an alternative explanation?). The resurrected Christ also appeared to five hundred eyewitnesses—too many people to dismiss the accounts as mass hysteria or the power of suggestion (1 Cor. 15:3-6).

Moreover, the original disciples refused to renounce Jesus, even though they were persecuted, tortured, and martyred. This

defeated band of men, who had already returned to their fishing
nets and boats, would never have been transformed into bold
preachers of the gospel and defenders of the faith had they not
seen Jesus' resurrected body and known him to be the living God.
Had they attempted a Passover plot, they could never have kept it
secret. People will die for something they *believe* to be true, but
they will never die for something they *know* to be false.

I know how impossible it is for a group of people, even some of
the most powerful in the world, to maintain a lie. The Watergate
cover-up lasted only a few weeks before the first conspirator broke
and turned state's evidence.[3]

A common stance, especially among theological liberals, is that
the historicity of Jesus' resurrection doesn't matter—that even
if the event didn't happen, Jesus is an important moral teacher.
India's late, great spiritual leader Mohandas Gandhi expressed
this attitude: "I may say that I have never been interested in an
historical Jesus. I should not care if it was proved by someone
that the man called Jesus never lived, and that what was narrated
in the Gospels was a figment of the writer's imagination. For the
Sermon on the Mount would still be true for me."[4]

But historical truth *does* matter. It is not enough to see Jesus'
death and resurrection as a symbol, a parable, a myth, a purely
subjective idea that can be "true for me," even if not true for others. The Christian message is the good news about what God has
done. *But if the gospel is a myth, then God has not done anything.*
"If religion be made independent of history, there is no such thing
as a gospel," wrote the great Christian scholar J. Gresham Machen.
"For 'gospel' means 'good news,' tidings, information about something that has happened. A gospel independent of history is a
contradiction in terms."[5]

Jesus' resurrection is much *more* than a historical fact, of course,
but it is nothing *less* than one. And the facts clearly support the
gospel's claims. Critics used to argue that the New Testament was

not written until hundreds of years after Jesus lived, by which time
a jungle of myth and legend had grown up and distorted the original events. But we now know that the New Testament books were
originally written a few decades after Christ's resurrection—far too
short a period for legends to develop. Even many liberal scholars
have come to agree that the New Testament was composed soon
after the recorded events occurred, at a time when many people
who knew Jesus were still alive and could dispute any false claims.
"In my opinion," writes William F. Albright, "every book of the
New Testament was written by a baptized Jew between the forties
and eighties of the first century." [6]

Moreover, we have several thousand copies of the New Testament, many of them very old. (Generally, the older the copy, the
closer it is to the original composition and therefore the more reliable it is considered to be.) Most of the New Testament books are
preserved in manuscripts that are dated only a little more than a
hundred years after the originals (and some fragments are dated
even earlier). By contrast, we have only twenty copies of the works
of the Roman writer Tacitus, and the earliest manuscript is dated
a thousand years after he lived. The earliest manuscript we have
of the work of Aristotle is dated fourteen hundred years after he
lived. The earliest copy of Caesar's *Gallic Wars* is dated a thousand
years after he wrote it. Yet no one questions either the historicity
of Tacitus or Aristotle or Caesar, or the authenticity of their writings.[7] The upshot is that today, Jesus' life is more thoroughly validated than that of virtually any other ancient figure.

The salvation attested to in the New Testament is the culmina-
tion of a long process of preparation in the Old Testament, which
is also historically reliable, as archeological discoveries continue to
confirm. For example, there was a time when critics said Moses
could not have written the Pentateuch because writing had not
yet been invented. Then archeologists discovered that writing was
well developed thousands of years before Moses' day. The Egyp-

tian and Babylonian cultures were highly literate cultures, with dictionaries, schools, and libraries.[8]

Critics once reserved their sharpest criticism for the early chapters of Genesis, dismissing the stories of the patriarchs as legend. But in recent years, archeological discoveries have repeatedly confirmed that Genesis gives highly accurate accounts of the names, places, trade routes, and customs of patriarchal times. Archeologists have found cuneiform tablets containing references to people such as Abraham and his brothers, Nahor and Haran. Tablets also explain puzzling customs, such as Abraham's and Jacob's practice of having children by a servant girl; the tablets show this was a common practice at the time. Yet, only a few centuries after the patriarchs lived, many of these names and practices and even some cities had completely disappeared. Contrary to what critics once claimed, it would have been impossible for the Bible writers to invent these stories later. They would have to have invented events that, by sheer chance, matched places and customs by then long forgotten.

The discovery of the Dead Sea Scrolls likewise provided confirmation for much of the Old Testament—even its supernatural character. Take Psalm 22, which predicts Christ's crucifixion in uncanny detail. Skeptics, rejecting the reality of divinely inspired prophecy, insisted that the psalm must have been written in the Maccabean Era, just before the birth of Christ, since before then, the practice of crucifixion did not exist in the Roman Empire. But when the Dead Sea Scrolls were discovered, they included copies of the Psalms dated centuries *before* the Maccabean Era.

And the evidence continues to mount. In the 1970s, archeological excavations confirmed the unique design of Philistine temples, with the roof supported by two central pillars about six feet apart. This discovery gives historical plausibility to the story of Samson, who grasped two pillars in the Philistine temple and brought it down.

Archeologists have also uncovered the ruins of the ancient city of Jericho and have found evidence that the walls of the city fell in an unusual manner—outward and flat, forming a perfect ramp for an invading army.[9] And in 1993, in Israel, archeologists uncovered a rock fragment inscribed with an ancient text referring to "the House of David," the first reference to King David and his royal family ever found outside the pages of the Bible.[10]

The historical data presses us to conclude that the stories in the Old and New Testaments are not made-up fables; they are accounts of real people and real events. As British journalist and historian Paul Johnson concludes, "It is not now the men of faith, it is the skeptics, who have reason to fear the course of discovery."[11]

THE MYTH BECOMES FACT

The old pagan world was littered with myths about a dying god who rises again, writes C. S. Lewis, but in Christianity, that myth became fact. "The dying god really appears—as a historical Person, living in a definite place and time."[12] Like a myth, the gospel is a colorful story that inspires our imagination, yet at the same time it is sober fact, something that happened in the real world. The story of Jesus, Lewis concludes, is "Perfect Myth and Perfect Fact: claiming not only our love and our obedience, but also our wonder and delight, addressed to the savage, the child, and the poet in each one of us no less than to the moralist, the scholar and the philosopher."[13]

But Christ's resurrection is only the beginning of the story of redemption. At Pentecost, the risen Christ sent forth the Holy Spirit into the lives of believers, to work out his purposes in their lives. Today as well, all believers receive the power to become children of God, to be transformed and restored to our true nature, people created in the image of God. And we live as the community of hope, in eschatological expectation, knowing that Christ will return and establish his rule over all.

God's redemption, then, does not change us into something different so much as it *restores* us to the way we were originally created. Virtually all of the words the Bible uses to describe salvation imply a return to something that originally existed. To *redeem* means to "buy back," and the image evokes a kidnapping: Someone pays the ransom and buys captives back, restoring them to their original freedom. *Reconciliation* implies a relationship torn by conflict, then returned to its original friendship. The New Testament also speaks of *renewal,* implying that something has been battered and torn, then restored to its pristine condition. *Regeneration* implies something returned to life after having died. As Al Wolters notes, "All these terms suggest a *restoration* of some good thing that was spoiled or lost."[14]

Being justified before God is a wonderful gift, yet it is just the beginning. Salvation empowers us to take up the task laid on the first human beings at the dawn of creation: to subdue the earth and extend the Creator's dominion over all of life.

Only Christianity provides true redemption—a restoration to our created state and the hope of eternal peace with God. No other worldview identifies the real problem: the stain of sin in our souls. No other worldview can set free a tormented soul like Bernard Nathanson—or like me and you.

And having been liberated from sin, we are empowered to help bring Christ's restoration to the entire creation order.

SESSION 6

DISCUSSION QUESTIONS

CHAPTER 14

1 What elements of Eastern religions are attractive to post-Christian Americans?

2 How do spiritual evolutionists view God? How do they view our human relationship or role in relation to God?

3 What evidence do you see of New Age beliefs in the media and in your community?

4 What answers does the New Age worldview give for the three major life questions?

5 Discuss what the phrase "just as I am" would mean to a New Ager. What does it mean to a Christian?

6 Read John 4:7-27, the account of Jesus' conversation with a

woman who was confused about religion, among other things. How did he turn a mundane conversation (which he initiated) into a spiritual discussion? Is this difficult for you to do? If so, why? Share examples of how you have done, or might do, this with neighbors.

7 Which of these three words best describes this John 4 encounter: *a conversation, a monologue,* or *a sermon*? In what other ways would you describe Jesus' approach? (Did he confront? Challenge? Was he direct or indirect? Brusque? Kind?) What can you learn from this passage about sharing the gospel with nonbelievers?

CHAPTER 15

8 In the Christian worldview, what is the most basic human problem? What solution does Christianity offer to this problem?

9 In contrast, briefly summarize the promise of redemption as offered by:

a. commercialism

b. neo-Marxism

c. sexual liberation

d. science and technology

e. New Age philosophy

10 Why is it important to stress that Christianity's solution is rooted in historical truth?

11 On a flip chart or board, list the cited archeological discoveries that confirm the reliability of the Bible. As a group, come up with an acronym that will help you remember the list, to bolster your credibility when talking with nonbelievers.

12 List and discuss the meaning of the Five Rs (use noun forms) presented at the end of the chapter. What do these nouns mean for you personally? For you as a group?

13 Read aloud Hebrews 2:5-9. Verses 6-8 quote from Psalm 8, describing the purpose for which we are restored in redemption. In what areas of your life are you consciously and consistently taking a "Psalm 8" approach—seeking to bring all things in line with God's purpose for creation? (Refer to Psalm 8 to gain more insight.)

14 What reality is described in verse 8? What greater reality is described in verse 9? What does this mean for you?

15 What difference does it make to you that God redeemed you through the death of his Son and promises you eternal life with him? Discuss this especially in the context of the title of part 2 of this book: "What can we do to fix it"—the broken world?

ROLE PLAY

Refer to the directions for role play at the end of session 1 (pp. 40–41).

CONVERSATION STARTERS

a. Assume that a neighbor claims, "It doesn't really matter whether Jesus lived—or rose from the dead. It's just a myth."

b. Assume a non-Christian friend opens the door wide, asking about your faith. "So, tell me: what is this Christianity line all about? . . . Jesus. Buddha. The Force. Isn't it all the same?" How would you explain the gospel message?

CLOSING SUMMARY

What is the one thing you want to remember from what you read (or heard or did) in this session?

Consider sharing this with the group.

WHAT'S AHEAD

T*he Problem of Evil* is the second in the three-part "Developing a Christian Worldview" series that addresses overarching world-view issues. We recommend that you continue your study with book 3: *The Christian in Today's Culture.* In six sessions this third book covers a fourth significant question: So how, now, shall we live out our Christian worldview?

Building on the material you've just read and studied in this book—addressing What has gone wrong with the world? and What can we do to fix it?—*The Christian in Today's Culture* discusses what it means to carry out the biblical mandates given to us as Christians. You'll find many real-life examples of Christians who are putting feet to their faith and transforming their families, schools, and neighborhoods as well as the arenas of economics, law and politics, science, the arts, music, and popular culture. This call to action and the related discussions will inspire you and equip you to become part of God's redeeming force in this new millennium.

NOTES

INTRODUCTION

1. Read the story of my conversion in *Born Again* (Old Tappan, N.J.: Chosen, 1976).
2. Abraham Kuyper, *Christianity: A Total World and Life System* (Marlborough, N.H.: Plymouth Rock Foundation, 1996), 39–40.
3. Ibid., 41.
4. Cornelius Plantinga Jr., "Fashions and Folly: Sin and Character in the 90s," (presented at the January Lecture Series, Calvin Theological Seminary, Grand Rapids, Michigan, January 15, 1993), 14–15.
5. Ibid.
6. Ibid.
7. Richard M. Weaver, *Ideas Have Consequences* (Chicago: University of Chicago Press, 1984).
8. Samuel Huntington, "The Clash of Civilizations," *Journal of Foreign Affairs* (summer 1993): 22. Huntington identified the major power blocs as the Western, Islamic, Chinese, Hindu, Orthodox, Japanese, and possibly African regions.
9. James Kurth, "The Real Clash of Civilization," *Washington Times,* 4 October 1994.
10. Jacques Toubon, cited in "Living with America," *Calgary Herald,* 6 October 1993.

CHAPTER 1
THE TROUBLE WITH US

1. Harold S. Kushner, *When Bad Things Happen to Good People* (New York: Schoken Books, 1980).
2. Edward T. Oakes, "Original Sin: A Disputation," *First Things* (November 1998): 21.
3. William F. Buckley Jr., *Nearer My God: An Autobiography of Faith* (New York: Doubleday, 1997), 232.

CHAPTER 2
A BETTER WAY OF LIVING?

1. David U. Gerstel, *Paradise, Incorporated: Synanon* (Novato, Calif.: Presidio Press, 1982), 36. In 1977, AA old-timers were often suspicious of younger people coming out of the drug culture. Today, Alcoholics Anonymous has branches called Narcotics Anonymous (NA) and Cocaine Anonymous (CA).
2. Synanon reached a $600,000 out-of-court settlement with the *San Francisco Examiner* in 1976. See Betsy Carter, Michael Reese, and Martin Kasindorf, *Newsweek* (November 20, 1978): 133. In addition to the Hearst settlement, Time, Inc. paid $2 million to defend itself against Synanon's libel suit. See Fred Barbash, "Alton Telegraph Libel Judgment Sends Fearful Message to Press," *Washington Post*, 25 August 1981. In the 1970s, Synanon sued the American Broadcasting Company for slander (against one of their radio programs). ABC paid Synanon $1.25 million to drop its suit. See Nanette Asimov, "Life after Synanon for Radio Veteran Dan Sorkin," *San Francisco Chronicle*, 1 May 1990.
3. William F. Olin, *Escape from Utopia: My Ten Years in Synanon* (Santa Cruz, Calif.: Unity Press, 1980), 209–11.
4. Gerstel, *Paradise*, 185.
5. Olin, *Escape from Utopia*, 247.
6. Gerstel, *Paradise*, 211. "Jean" is based on a woman who was five months pregnant at the time of Dederich's pronouncement and who submitted to an abortion.
7. Gerstel, *Paradise*, 216–24.
8. Some states sent offenders to Synanon as an alternative to state-run correctional facilities.
9. In a recording made from "the Wire," which later became key evidence in the critical case against Synanon, Dederich declared these and other violent intentions. See Gerstel, *Paradise*, 268.
10. Gerstel, *Paradise*, 244.
11. A few "deadbeats" who had voiced criticisms of Dederich's "emotional surgery" were forced into the Mojave Desert to load rocks into wheelbarrows under the scorching sun. At night they huddled together in a tent, trying to stave off hypothermia. Fortunately, after only nine days of this, an heiress who was putting much of her wealth into Synanon visited the camp and objected to the conditions. The workday was shortened, decent quarters were built, and the fact that it was still a forced-labor camp was muted. See Gerstel, *Paradise*, 236–37.

12. "Kenton Son Sought in Snake-Bite of Anti-Synanon Lawyer," *Washington Post,* 13 October 1978.

CHAPTER 3
SYNANON AND SIN

1. Glenn Tinder, *Political Thinking: The Perennial Questions* (New York: HarperCollins, 1995), 199.
2. Ralph Waldo Emerson, as quoted in Roger Lundin, *The Culture of Interpretation: Christian Faith and the Postmodern World* (Grand Rapids: Eerdmans, 1993), 111.
3. Glenn Tinder, "Birth of a Troubled Conscience," *Christianity Today* (April 26, 1999): 37.
4. Karl Menninger, *Whatever Became of Sin?* (New York: Hawthorn Books, 1973).
5. Jean-Jacques Rousseau, *The Social Contract* (Boston: Charles E. Tuttle, Everyman's Classic Library, 1993), 181.
6. Jean-Jacques Rousseau, as quoted in Robert Nisbet, *The Quest for Community: A Study in the Ethics of Order and Freedom* (San Francisco: ICS Press, 1990), 127. As Nisbet explains, Rousseau felt that "the State is the means by which the individual can be freed of the restrictive tyrannies that compose society" (*The Quest for Community,* 128).
7. Tinder, *Political Thinking,* 200.
8. Nisbet, *The Quest for Community,* 127.
9. Historian Glenn Tinder puts it well: "Political leaders claim that power that the Old Testament attributes to God alone—that of erasing and avenging all injustice and of guiding humanity to its destined fulfillment" (Tinder, *Political Thinking,* 201).
10. Rousseau, *The Social Contract,* 275.
11. Ibid., 195.
12. Friedrich Nietzsche, *The Birth of Tragedy* and the *Genealogy of Morals,* trans. Francis Golffing (New York: Doubleday, 1956), 277–78.
13. Edward T. Oakes, "Original Sin: A Disputation," *First Things* (November 1998): 16.
14. Paul Johnson, *Intellectuals* (New York: Harper & Row, 1988), 22–23.
15. Jean-Jacques Rousseau, *Confessions,* vol. 1 (New York: Dutton, 1904), 314.
16. Ibid., 316.
17. Rousseau, as quoted in Paul Johnson, *Intellectuals,* 22.
18. Will Durant and Ariel Durant, *Rousseau and Revolution: A History*

of Civilization in France, England, and Germany from 1756, and in the Remainder of Europe from 1715 to 1789, vol. 10 of *The Story of Civilization* (New York: Simon & Schuster, 1967), 886.

CHAPTER 4
WE'RE ALL UTOPIANS NOW

1. Alexis de Tocqueville, *Democracy in America,* trans. George Lawrence, Great Books of the Western World, ed. Mortimer Adler (Chicago: Encyclopedia Britannica, 1991), 374–77.
2. Nancy R. Pearcey and Charles B. Thaxton, *The Soul of Science: Christian Faith and Natural Philosophy* (Wheaton, Ill.: Crossway, 1994), 71–73.
3. The following discussion about Freud, Fechner, and Pavlov is based on "Evolution and the Humanities," a presentation made by Willem J. Ouweneel at the National Creation Conference, August 1985. See also Nancy R. Pearcey, "Sensible Psychology: How Creation Makes the Difference," *Bible-Science Newsletter* (February 1996): 7.
4. B. F. Skinner, *Walden Two* (New York: Macmillan, 1976).
5. J. B. Watson, *The Way of Behaviorism* (New York: Harper, 1928), 35ff.
6. John B. Watson, *Behaviorism* (New York: The People's Institute, 1924), 248. American philosopher and educator John Dewey used even stronger utopian language, heralding the teacher as "the prophet of the true God and the usherer in of the true kingdom of God" (John Dewey, *My Pedagogic Creed* [Washington, D.C.: The Progressive Education Association, 1929], 17).
7. Dean Koontz, as quoted in Nick Gillespie and Lisa Snell, "Contemplating Evil: Novelist Dean Koontz on Freud, Fraud, and the Great Society," *Reason* 28, no. 6 (November 1996): 44.
8. Mike Swift, "Raising Hopes by Razing Housing," *Hartford Courant,* 19 March 1995.
9. Ramsey Clark, *Crime in America: Observations on Its Nature, Causes, Prevention, and Control* (New York: Simon & Schuster, 1970), 17–18.
10. Clarence Darrow, *Attorney for the Damned,* ed. Arthur Weinberg (New York: Simon & Schuster, 1957), 3–4.
11. Myron Magnet, *The Dream and the Nightmare: The Sixties' Legacy to the Underclass* (New York: William Morrow, 1993), 197–98. Moreover, evidence from social science shows this approach to be

wrong. In the 1950s, Samuel Yochelson, a psychiatrist, and Stanton Samenow, a psychologist, set out to prove the conventional wisdom that crime is caused by such environmental forces as poverty and racism. But at the end of their seventeen-year study, they concluded that crime cannot be traced to social or economic causes. Instead, in every case the criminal act "was the product of deliberation." In short, the person "made choices." In their book *The Criminal Personality* they say that the answer to crime and the criminal personality is a "conversion to a whole new [responsible] lifestyle" (Samuel Yochelson and Stanton E. Samenow, *The Criminal Personality: A Profile for Change,* vol. 1 [New York: Jason Aronson, 1982], 19–20, 36).

12. John Leo, "The It's-Not-My-Fault Syndrome," *U.S. News and World Report* 108, no. 24 (June 18, 1990): 16.

13. George Flynn, "Woman Sues Houston Nightclub over Hot-Dog Eating Contest," *Houston Chronicle,* 25 March 1997. Victoria Franks Rios dropped her suit against the nightclub in December 1997. See George Flynn, "Woman Drops Her Lawsuit over Hot-Dog Eating Event," *Houston Chronicle,* 23 December 1997.

14. C. S. Lewis, "The Humanitarian Theory of Punishment," *God in the Dock* (Grand Rapids: Eerdmans, 1970), 292.

15. Ibid.

CHAPTER 5
THE FACE OF EVIL

1. Tammy Busche, "Parents Question Security in Wake of Student Arrests in Shooting Plot," *St. Louis Post-Dispatch,* 28 May 98.

2. "Police Seek Onlookers Who Cheered Killer," *Naples Daily News,* 15 August 1993.

3. Ed Hayward, "Second Teen Suspect to Be Tried," *Boston Herald,* 25 September 1994.

4. Karl Vick, "Delaware Seeks Death Penalty against Teens in Infant's Death," *Washington Post,* 19 November 1996.

5. Arianna Huffington, "Amy and Brian's Shameful Excuse Factory," *New York Post,* 14 July 1998.

6. Ron Rosenbaum, "Staring into the Heart of the Heart of Darkness," *New York Times Magazine* (June 4, 1995): 36.

7. *The New England Primer* (Hartford, Conn.: John Babcock, 1800).

8. Benjamin Spock, as quoted in Dana Mack, *The Assault on Parent-*

    hood: How Our Culture Undermines the Family (New York: Simon & Schuster, 1997), 33.

9. Haim G. Ginott, *Between Parent and Child: New Solutions to Old Problems* (New York: Macmillan, 1965); and Thomas Gordon, *P.E.T., Parent Effectiveness Training: The No-lose Program for Raising Responsible Children* (New York: P. H. Wyden, 1975).

10. For Spock "the 'good' parent was no longer the parent who got his children to behave, but rather the parent who understood why his children might not behave" (Mack, *The Assault on Parenthood*, 33).

11. "Seven Deadly Sins," MTV (August 1993).

12. Alan Bullock, as quoted in Charles Maier, a review of *Hitler and Stalin: Parallel Lives*, by Alan Bullock, *New Republic* (June 15, 1992): 42.

13. Thomas Harris, *The Silence of the Lambs* (New York: St. Martin's Press, 1988), 19 (emphasis in the original).

14. Bruno Bettelheim, *The Uses of Enchantment: The Meaning and Importance of Fairy Tales* (New York: Alfred A. Knopf, 1977).

15. Susan Wise Bauer, "Stephen King's Tragic Kingdom," *Books & Culture* (March/April 1997): 14.

16. Nick Gillespie and Lisa Snell, "Contemplating Evil: Novelist Dean Koontz on Freud, Fraud, and the Great Society," *Reason* 28, no. 6 (November 1996): 44.

CHAPTER 6
A SNAKE IN THE GARDEN

1. Personal conversation with Nancy Pearcey (May 22, 1997).

2. Such a philosophy was held by an ancient Persian religion called Manichaeism, which taught that good and evil are both eternal principles, locked in an eternal conflict in which neither would ever triumph.

3. See Job 1 and 2, for example. Beginning in the New Testament, Satan is referred to as "the devil."

4. Francis A. Schaeffer, *Genesis in Space and Time* (Downers Grove, Ill.: InterVarsity Press, 1972), 80–83.

5. C. S. Lewis, *The Discarded Image: An Introduction to Medieval and Renaissance Literature* (Cambridge: Cambridge University Press, 1994), 155.

6. Dennis Prager, as quoted in "Religious Right Takes Heat for Salting and Lighting Cultural Debate," *Orlando Sentinel*, 26 August 1995.

7. James Madison, *The Federalist*, no. 48 (February 1, 1788).

CHAPTER 7
DOES SUFFERING MAKE SENSE?

1. While we tell this story about Einstein, Hertzen, McNaughton, and Hartman in a fictionalized dramatic form, it accurately represents Einstein's published views. The key ideas in this story are based on two books: Albert Einstein, *Out of My Later Years: The Scientist, Philosopher, and Man Portrayed through His Own Words* (Princeville, Ore.: Bonanza Books, 1990), 30–33; and Albert Einstein, *The World As I See It,* trans. Alan Harris (New York: Citadel Press, 1995), 24–29.

2. Spinoza was a seventeenth-century philosopher who used the word *God* to refer simply to the principle of order in the universe. See Robert Jastrow, *God and the Astronomers* (New York: Warner Books, 1980), 17.

3. This idea is expressed in Einstein, *Out of My Later Years,* 30–33; and *The World As I See It,* 24–29.

4. Ibid.

5. Ibid.

6. Albert Einstein, *Science, Philosophy, and Religion: A Symposium,* (New York: The Conference on Science, Philosophy, and Religion in Their Relation to the Democratic Way of Life, Inc., 1941).

7. Gerald Holton and Yehuda Elkana, *Albert Einstein: Historical and Cultural Perspectives* (Princeton, N.J.: Princeton University Press, 1982), 209.

8. Albert Einstein, as quoted in Ronald W. Clark, *Einstein: The Life and Times, An Illustrated Biography* (New York: Wings Books, 1995), 19.

9. Einstein, *The World As I See It,* 27–29.

10. Ibid., 24–29.

11. Jastrow, *God and the Astronomers,* 17.

12. Stephen Crane, as quoted in James W. Sire, *The Universe Next Door: A Basic Worldview Catalog,* 3rd ed. (Downers Grove, Ill.: InterVarsity Press, 1997), 13.

13. Glenn Tinder, "Birth of a Troubled Conscience," *Christianity Today* (April 26, 1999): 30.

14. Paul Helm, "Faith and Reason: Stained with the Blood of Suffering," *The Independent,* 23 April 1994.

15. Harold S. Kushner, *When Bad Things Happen to Good People* (New York: Schoken Books, 1981), 42–43.

16. John Hick, *Evil and the God of Love* (London: Collins, 1968).

17. Archibald MacLeish, *J. B.: A Play in Verse* (Boston: Houghton Mifflin, 1958), 126.

18. Fyodor Dostoyevsky, as quoted in Peter Kreeft, *Making Sense out of Suffering* (Ann Arbor, Mich.: Servant, 1986), 8.

19. Ibid., 9.

20. Norman Geisler and Ronald Brooks, *When Skeptics Ask: A Handbook of Christian Evidence* (Wheaton, Ill.: Victor, 1998), chapter 4.

21. *The Martyrdom of the Holy Polycarp*, as cited in Eberhard Arnold, *The Early Christians: After the Death of the Apostles* (Rifton, N.Y.: Plough, 1972), 66.

22. Friedrich Nietzsche, as quoted in Melvin Tinker, *Why Do Bad Things Happen to Good People?: A Biblical Look at the Problem of Suffering* (Fearn, UK: Christian Focus, 1997), 4.

23. Saint Augustine, *Enchiridon*, 27, as quoted in *The Book of Catholic Quotations*, ed. John Chapin (New York: Farrar, Straus and Cudahy, 1956), 313.

CHAPTER 8
GOOD INTENTIONS

1. This story is a dramatic reconstruction based on a true event. Dr. Nathanson did abort one of his own children, and in our interview with him he described his attitude throughout as cold and clinical. In *The Hand of God* he writes: "The procedure went on without incident, and I felt a fleeting gratification that I had done my usual briskly efficient job and left the operating room while she was still struggling up from general anesthesia. Yes, you may ask me: That was a concise terse report of what you *did,* but what did you feel? Did you not feel sad—not only because you had extinguished the life of an unborn child, but, more, because you had destroyed your *own* child? I swear to you that I had no feelings aside from the sense of accomplishment, the pride of expertise. On inspecting the contents of the bag, I felt only the satisfaction of knowing that I had done a thorough job. You pursue me: You ask if perhaps for a fleeting moment or so I experienced a flicker of regret, a microgram of remorse? No and no. And that, dear reader, is the mentality of the abortionist: another job well done, another demonstration of the moral neutrality of advanced technology in the hands of the amoral" (Bernard N. Nathanson, *The Hand of God: A Journey from Death to Life by the Abortion Doctor Who Changed His Mind* [Washington, D.C.: Regnery, 1996], 58–61 [emphasis in the original]).

2. This ultrasound scene is a composite of many experiences Dr. Nathanson had with ultrasound scans. While this is an accurate description of the impact of that first ultrasound on Nathanson, it also incorporates recent technology. Nathanson would not have been able to see quite this much with the first ultrasound machines.

3. Bernard N. Nathanson, "Sounding Board, Deeper into Abortion," *New England Journal of Medicine* 291, no. 22 (November 28, 1974): 1188–90.

4. The colleague who performed the procedures that day later saw the tapes and vowed he would never again do another abortion.

5. *The Silent Scream* can be viewed on-line at http:// www.silentscream.org or can be ordered from American Portrait Films, 503 East 200th Street, Cleveland, OH 44119, phone: (216) 531-8600.

6. Bernard N. Nathanson, *Why I'm Still Catholic*, ed. Kevin and Marilyn Ryan (New York: Riverhead Books, 1998), 281.

7. Augustine, *Confessions* (New York: Penguin, 1961), 151, 170.

8. Nathanson, *The Hand of God*, 187–88, 195–96.

9. Ibid., 193.

10. Nathanson, *Why I'm Still Catholic*, 282.

CHAPTER 9
IN SEARCH OF REDEMPTION

1. Dorothy L. Sayers, *Creed or Chaos* (Manchester, N.H.: Sophia Institute Press, 1974), chapter 3.

2. James B. Twitchell, *Adcult U.S.A.: The Triumph of Advertising in American Culture* (New York: Columbia University Press, 1996), 38.

3. Ibid.

4. Ibid., 45.

5. Jennifer Harrison, "Advertising Joins the Journey of the Soul," *American Demographics* (June 1997): 22.

6. John Updike, as quoted in Twitchell, *Adcult U.S.A.*, vii.

7. Calvin Coolidge, as quoted in Twitchell, *Adcult U.S.A.*, vii.

CHAPTER 10
DOES IT LIBERATE?

1. Mary Midgley, *Evolution as a Religion: Strange Hopes and Stranger Fears* (New York: Methuen, 1985), 30–35. This chapter draws

extensively on Nancy R. Pearcey, "Religion of Revolution: Karl
Marx's Social Evolution," *Bible-Science Newsletter* (June 1986): 7.

2. Nancy R. Pearcey and Charles B. Thaton, *The Soul of Science:
Christian Faith and Natural Philosophy* (Wheaton, Ill.: Crossway
Books, 1994), 107.

3. Vladimir Lenin, as quoted in Francis Nigel Lee, *Communism versus
Creation* (Nutley, N.J.: Craig Press, 1969), 28.

4. Robert Wesson, *Why Marxism? The Continuing Success of a Failed
Theory* (New York: Basic Books, 1976), 30.

5. Throughout their lives, Marx and his colleague Frederick Engels
looked expectantly for the *Dies Irae,* as they themselves called it,
when the mighty would be cast down. The *Dies Irae* (literally "day of
wrath") is a medieval Latin hymn about the Day of Judgment and is
sung in requiem masses.

6. Klaus Bockmuehl, *The Challenge of Marxism* (Leicester, England:
InterVarsity Press, 1980), 17.

7. Modern historians do not accept Marx's stages of social and
economic evolution—from primitive communism to slavery to
serfdom to capitalism to communism.

8. Paul Johnson, *Intellectuals,* (New York: Harper & Row, 1988), 53,
56.

9. Karl Marx and Frederick Engels, "Private Property and Communism," in *Collected Works,* vol. 3 (New York: International Publishers,
1975), 304 (emphasis in the original).

10. Ibid.

11. Karl Marx, as quoted in Thomas Sowell, *Marxism* (New York:
William Morrow, 1985), 166.

12. Bernard-Henri Levi, as quoted in Ronald Nash, *Social Justice and the
Christian Church* (Milford, Mich.: Mott Media, 1983), 102.

CHAPTER 11
SALVATION THROUGH SEX?

1. Madison Jones, *An Exile* (Savannah, Ga.: Frederic C. Beil, 1990),
56.

2. Margaret Sanger, *The Pivot of Civilization* (New York: Brentanos,
1922), 238–39. This section draws heavily on Nancy R. Pearcey,
"Creating the 'New Man': The Hidden Agenda in Sex Education,"
Bible-Science Newsletter (May 1990): 6.

3. Ibid., 232.

4. Ibid.

5. Ibid., 233.

6. Ibid., 270–71.

7. Alfred C. Kinsey, *Sexual Behavior in the Human Male* (Philadelphia: W. B. Saunders, 1948); and Alfred C. Kinsey, *Sexual Behavior in the Human Female* (Bloomington, Ind.: Indiana University Press, 1998).

8. Kinsey, *Sexual Behavior in the Human Male,* 59.

9. Alan Wolf, review of *Alfred C. Kinsey: A Public/Private Life,* by James H. Jones, *New Republic* 217, no. 21 (November 24, 1997): 31.

10. Paul Robinson, *The Modernization of Sex* (New York: Cornell University Press, 1988), 83–86.

11. Wilhelm Reich, as quoted in Eustace Chesser, *Salvation through Sex: The Life and Work of Wilhelm Reich* (New York: William Morrow, 1973), 44.

12. Wilhelm Reich, *Ether, God and Devil: Cosmic Superimposition* (New York: Farrar, Straus and Giroux, 1973), 9.

13. Chesser, *Salvation through Sex,* 67.

14. Robert Rimmer, *The Harrad Experiment* (Amherst, N.Y.: Prometheus Books, 1990), 13, 46, 145.

15. Ibid., 157, 167.

16. Ibid., 264.

17. Mary Calderone, "Sex Education and the Roles of School and Church," *The Annals of the American Academy of Political and Social Sciences* 376 (March 1968): 57.

18. Mary S. Calderone and Eric W. Johnson, *The Family Book about Sexuality* (New York: Harper & Row, 1981), 171.

19. Calderone, "Sex Education," 59.

20. Madeline Gray, *Margaret Sanger: A Biography of the Champion of Birth Control* (New York: Richard Marek, 1979), 416–18.

21. James H. Jones, "Annals of Sexology," *New Yorker* (August 25, 1997): 98.

22. Judith A. Reisman and Edward W. Eichel, *Kinsey, Sex, and Fraud: The Indoctrination of a People* (Lafayette, La.: Huntington House, 1990), 29–30.

23. Chesser, *Salvation through Sex,* 71.

CHAPTER 12
IS SCIENCE OUR SAVIOR?

1. *Independence Day,* Twentieth Century Fox (1996).

2. *War of the Worlds,* Paramount Pictures (1953).

3. Daniel Quinn, *Ishmael* (New York: Bantam Books, 1992).

4. Francis Bacon, as quoted in John Herman Randall, *The Making of the Modern Mind* (New York: Columbia University Press, 1976), 204.

5. See Auguste Comte, *Religion of Humanity: The Positivist Calendar of Auguste Comte, and other Tables* (London: The London Positivist Society, 1929); and Auguste Comte, *The Religion of Humanity: Love, Order, Progress, Live for Others, Live Openly* (Liverpool, England: Church of Humanity, 1907). See also T. R. Wright, *The Religion of Humanity: The Impact of Comtean Positivism on Victorian Britain* (Cambridge: Cambridge University Press, 1986).

6. Mary Midgley, *Evolution as a Religion: Strange Hopes and Stranger Fears* (New York: Nethuen and Co., 1985), 34. Ironically, Darwin himself admitted that he could see "no innate tendency to progressive development."

7. Ian Barbour, *Issues in Science and Religion* (New York: Harper Torchbooks, 1966), 94.

8. J. D. Bernal, as quoted in Mary Midgley, *Evolution as a Religion*, 35.

9. H. J. Muller, as quoted in Mary Midgley, *Evolution as a Religion*, 34.

10. Francis Crick, *Life Itself, Its Origin and Nature* (New York: Simon & Schuster, 1981), 118.

11. Oliver O'Donovan, *Begotten or Made?* (London: Oxford University Press, 1984).

12. Beyond this, when you consider that the supposed evolutionary process requires several million years to accomplish even minor changes, the idea that we can predict anything at all about the end result is preposterous. This is utter pie-in-the-sky, blind faith.

13. Stephen Hawking, *A Brief History in Time* (New York: Bantam Books, 1988).

14. Frank Drake, interviewed by Bob Arnold in "Frank Drake Assesses the NASA Search," *SETI News* (first quarter, 1993).

15. Carl Sagan, *Broca's Brain* (New York: Random, 1979), 276.

16. Ibid.

17. Cited in Terence Dickinson, "Critics Scoff but Cool ET Hunt Carries On," *Toronto Star*, 24 August 1997.

18. Sagan, *Broca's Brain*, 276.

CHAPTER 13
THE DRAMA OF DESPAIR

1. Steven Weinberg, *The First Three Minutes: A Modern View of the Origin of the Universe* (London: André Deutsch, 1977), 155.

2. Ibid., 1–2.

3. Jean-Paul Sartre, *No Exit and Three Other Plays* (New York: Random, 1949).

4. Albert Camus, *The Myth of Sisyphus and Other Essays* (New York: Alfred A. Knopf, 1955).

5. Lord Balfour, as quoted in John Herman Randall, *The Making of the Modern Mind* (New York: Columbia University Press, 1940), 581–82.

6. Randall, *The Making of the Modern Mind*, 581–82 (emphasis added).

7. Bertrand Russell, as quoted in Randall, *The Making of the Modern Mind*, 582.

8. Jacques Monod, *Chance and Necessity*, trans. Austryn Wainhouse (London: Fontana, 1974), 160.

9. Michael T. Ghiselin, *The Economy of Nature and the Evolution of Sex* (Berkeley, Calif.: University of California Press, 1974), 247.

10. Mark Ridley, *The Origins of Virtue: Human Instincts and the Revolution of Cooperation* (New York: Viking, 1996).

11. Ibid.

12. Richard Dawkins, *The Selfish Gene* (London: Oxford University Press, 1976), 2–3.

13. Edward O. Wilson, *Sociobiology: The New Synthesis* (Cambridge, Mass.: Harvard University Press, 1975), 3.

14. Dawkins, *The Selfish Gene*, 2–3.

15. Ibid., 2, 64 (emphasis added).

16. Mary Midgley, *Evolution as a Religion: Strange Hopes and Stranger Fears*, (New York: Nethuen and Co., 1985), 131, 140. See also Nancy R. Pearcey, "What Do You Mean: 'Evolution Is a Religion'?" *Bible-Science Newsletter* (April 1988): 7.

17. Edward O. Wilson, as quoted in Howard L. Kaye, *The Social Meaning of Modern Biology* (New Haven: Yale University Press, 1986), 169–79.

18. Ibid.

19. Brendan I. Koerner, "Extreeeme," *U.S. News and World Report* (June 30, 1997): 50.

20. Kristen Ulmer, as quoted in Koerner, "Extreeeme," 50.

21. "NBC Nightly News" (June 19, 1998).

22. "Hero of the Code," *Time* (July 14, 1961): 87.

23. See chapter 2 in Colson's *Kingdoms in Conflict* (New York: William Morrow; Grand Rapids: Zondervan, 1987).

24. Saint Augustine, *Confessions*, book 1, paragraph 1, trans. R. S. Pine-Coffin (New York: Penguin, 1961), 21.

CHAPTER 14
THAT NEW AGE RELIGION

1. R. Ascher-Walsch, et al., "October," *Entertainment Weekly* (August 22, 1997).
2. K. K. Campbell, "Getting Your Kicks on the Net," *Toronto Star*, 29 May 1997.
3. *Hair* opened off Broadway in 1967, then made its Broadway debut in 1968.
4. Ken Wilber, as quoted in Robert Burrows, "New Age Movement: Self-Deification in a Secular Culture," *Spiritual Counterfeit Project Newsletter* 10 (winter 1984–1985).
5. John Herman Randall, *The Making of the Modern Mind* (New York: Columbia University Press, 1976), 419.
6. Alfred, Lord Tennyson, *In Memoriam*, LV–LVI.
7. For a discussion of these ideas, see Randall, *The Making of the Modern Mind* and Ian Barbour, *Issues in Science and Religion* (New York: Harper Torchbooks, 1966).
8. Robert Lindsey, "Spiritual Concepts Drawing a Different Breed of Adherent," *New York Times*, 29 September 1986.
9. Martha M. Hamilton and Frank Swoboda, "Mantra for a Company Man: New Age Approaches Increasingly Popular in Management Training," *Washington Post*, 30 June 1996.
10. For example, yoga is sold as a means of relaxation or physical exercise. Yet the word *yoga* literally means "yoke," and the actual purpose of the exercise is to yoke, merge, or unite the individual spirit with the Cosmic Spirit.
11. Jill Anderson, *PUMSY in Pursuit of Excellence* (Eugene, Oreg.: Timberline Press, 1987).
12. Ibid.
13. Deborah Rozman writes in *Meditating with Children:* "Meditation takes us back to the Source of all Life. We become one with ALL." What PUMSY teaches coyly, Rozman teaches openly: that we all are God, that salvation consists in realizing our divine nature. She even encourages children to apply biblical phrases to themselves, such as "I and my Father are one," "Before Abraham was, I am," and "I am that I am." Deborah Rozman, *Meditating with Children: The Art of Concentration and Centering* (Boulder Creek, Calif.: Planetary Publishing, 1994), 143.
14. James Redfield, *The Tenth Insight: Holding the Vision* (New York: Warner Books, 1996). The same views were expressed in Redfield's

earlier best-seller, *The Celestine Prophecy: An Adventure* (New York: Warner Books, 1993), in which God is described as a "universal energy source" or the "Higher Will."

15. Frances Hodgson Burnett, *The Secret Garden* (New York: Dell, 1987), 230.

16. Ibid., 233.

17. Ibid., 230.

18. Ibid., 229.

19. Ibid., 233.

20. Peter Kreeft, *Fundamentals of the Faith: Essays in Christian Apologetics* (San Francisco: Ignatius Press, 1988), 90.

21. *Spiritual Counterfeit Project Newsletter* 10 (winter 1984–85).

22. Shirley MacLaine's television miniseries *Out on a Limb,* which aired in 1987, was based on her book *Out on a Limb* (New York: Bantam Books, 1983).

23. C. S. Lewis, *Miracles: A Preliminary Study* (London: Fount, 1974), 86–87.

24. Jennifer Caternini, "Feminists Still 'Re-Imagining' God," *Faith and Freedom* 16 (fall 1996): 6.

25. Kreeft, *Fundamentals of the Faith,* 93.

CHAPTER 15
REAL REDEMPTION

1. Ronald Knox, as quoted in Peter Kreeft, *Fundamentals of the Faith: Essays in Christian Apologetics* (San Francisco: Ignatius Press, 1988), 74.

2. While it is difficult to pinpoint the exact date of Christ's crucifixion, most biblical scholars agree that it is either A.D. 30 or A.D. 29. For information about the dating of Jesus' birth, see William Hendriksen, *The Gospel of Luke* (Grand Rapids: Baker, 1993), 139–41.

3. For a fuller explanation of this argument, referring to the Watergate cover-up, see Colson, "Watergate and the Resurrection," chapter 6 in *Loving God* (Grand Rapids: Zondervan, 1983).

4. Mohandas Gandhi, "Address on Christmas Day, 1931," as quoted in A. R. Vidler, *Objections to Christian Belief* (London: Constable, 1963), 59.

5. J. Gresham Machen, *Christianity and Liberalism* (New York: Macmillan, 1923), 121.

6. William F. Albright, as quoted in Norman L. Geisler, "Toward a

More Conservative View," *Baker Encyclopedia of Christian Apologetics* (Grand Rapids: Baker, 1999), 529.

7. Paul Johnson, "A Historian Looks at Jesus," (a speech first presented at Dallas Theological Seminary in 1986), *Sources,* no. 1 (1991).

8. Joseph P. Free, "Archaeology and Biblical Criticism," *Bibliotheca Sacra*
(January 1957): 23. See also Joseph P. Free, *Archaeology and Bible History* (Grand Rapids: Zondervan, 1992).

9. Charles R. Pellegrino, *Return to Sodom and Gomorrah: Bible Stories from Archaeologists* (New York: Random, 1994).

10. John Noble Wilford, "From Israeli Site, News of House of David," *New York Times,* 6 August 1993.

11. Johnson, "A Historian Looks at Jesus," *Sources,* no. 1 (1991).

12. C. S. Lewis, *God in the Dock: Essays on Theology and Ethics* (Grand Rapids: Eerdmans, 1970), 58.

13. Ibid., 67.

14. Al Wolters, *Creation Regained: Biblical Basics for a Reformational Worldview* (Grand Rapids: Eerdmans, 1985), 58 (emphasis in the original).

RECOMMENDED READING

WORLDVIEW

Bellah, Robert. *The Good Society*. New York: Alfred A. Knopf, 1991.

Berger, Peter, and Brigitte Berger, and Hansfried Kellner. *The Homeless Mind: Modernization and Consciousness*. New York: Random, 1974.

Blamires, Harry. *The Christian Mind*. Ann Arbor, Mich.: Servant, 1978.

Brown, Harold O. J. *The Sensate Culture*. Dallas: Word, 1996.

Carson, D. A., and John D. Woodbridge, eds. *God and Culture: Essays in Honor of Carl F. H. Henry*. Grand Rapids: Eerdmans, 1993.

Colson, Charles, with Anne Morse. *Burden of Truth: Defending Truth in an Age of Unbelief*. Wheaton, Ill.: Tyndale House, 1997.

Colson, Charles, with Nancy Pearcey. *A Dance with Deception: Revealing the Truth Behind the Headlines*. Dallas: Word, 1993.

Colson, Charles, with Ellen Santilli Vaughn. *The Body*. Dallas: Word, 1992.

Dawson, Christopher. *Religion and the Rise of Western Culture*. New York: Doubleday, 1991.

Dockery, David S., ed. *The Challenge of Postmodernism: An Evangelical Engagement*. Grand Rapids: Baker, 1997.

Dooyeweerd, Hermann. *Roots of Western Culture: Pagan, Secular, and Christian Options*. Toronto: Wedge, 1979.

———. *In the Twilight of Western Thought: Studies in the Pretended Autonomy of Philosophical Thought*. Lewiston, N.Y.: E. Mellen, 1999.

Eliot, T. S. *Christianity and Culture*. New York: Harcourt, Brace and Jovanovich, 1968.

Geisler, Norman L., and Ronald M. Brooks. *When Skeptics Ask: A Handbook of Christian Evidence*. Wheaton, Ill.: Victor, 1998.

Glover, Willis B. *Biblical Origins of Modern Secular Culture: An Essay in the Interpretation of Western History*. Macon, Ga.: Mercer University Press, 1984.

Grisez, Germain G. *The Way of the Lord Jesus.* Vol. 1, *Christian Moral Principles.* Chicago: Franciscan Herald Press, 1983.

———. *The Way of the Lord Jesus.* Vol. 2, *Living a Christian Life.* Quincy, Ill.: Franciscan Press, 1993.

———. *The Way of the Lord Jesus.* Vol. 3, *Difficult Moral Questions.* Quincy, Ill.: Franciscan Press, 1997.

Gunton, Colin. *Enlightenment and Alienation: An Essay Toward a Trinitarian Theology.* Grand Rapids: Eerdmans, 1985.

Halton, Eugene. *Bereft of Reason: On the Decline of Social Thought and Prospects for Its Renewal.* Chicago: University of Chicago Press, 1995.

Henry, Carl F. H. *The Christian Mind-set in a Secular Society: Promoting Evangelical Renewal and National Righteousness.* Portland, Ore.: Multnomah, 1978.

Heslam, Peter S. *Creating a Christian Worldview: Abraham Kuyper's Lectures on Calvinism.* Grand Rapids: Eerdmans, 1998.

Hoffecker, W. Andrew, and Gary Scott Smith, eds. *Building a Christian Worldview.* Vol. 1, *God, Man, and Knowledge.* Phillipsburg, N.J.: Presbyterian and Reformed, 1986.

Holmes, Arthur. *All Truth Is God's Truth.* Grand Rapids: Eerdmans, 1977.

Holmes, Arthur, ed. *The Making of a Christian Mind: A Christian World View & the Academic Enterprise.* Downers Grove, Ill.: InterVarsity Press, 1985.

Kuyper, Abraham. *Christianity: A Total World and Life System.* Marlborough, N.H.: Plymouth Rock Foundation, 1996.

Machen, J. Gresham. *Christianity and Liberalism.* Grand Rapids: Eerdmans, 1990.

Moreland, J. P. *Love Your God with All Your Mind: The Role of Reason in the Life of the Soul.* Colorado Springs: NavPress, 1997.

Noll, Mark. *The Scandal of the Evangelical Mind.* Downers Grove, Ill.: InterVarsity Press, 1994.

Runner, H. Evan. *The Relation of the Bible to Learning.* Toronto: Wedge, 1970.

Schaeffer, Francis. *The Complete Works of Francis A. Schaeffer: A Christian Worldview.* Westchester, Ill.: Crossway, 1982.

———. *25 Basic Bible Studies: Including Two Contents, Two Realities.*

Wheaton, Ill.: Crossway, 1996. Also in *The Complete Works of Francis A. Schaeffer: A Christian Worldview*. Vol. 3, *A Christian View of Spirituality*. Westchester, Ill.: Crossway, 1982.

———. *Art and the Bible*. Downers Grove, Ill.: InterVarsity Press, 1973. Also in *The Complete Works of Francis A. Schaeffer: A Christian Worldview*. Vol. 2, *A Christian View of the Bible as Truth*. Westchester, Ill.: Crossway, 1982.

———. *Back to Freedom and Dignity*. In *The Complete Works of Francis A. Schaeffer: A Christian Worldview*. Vol. 1, *A Christian View of Philosophy and Culture*. Westchester, Ill.: Crossway, 1982.

———. *Basic Bible Studies*. In *The Complete Works of Francis A. Schaeffer: A Christian Worldview*. Vol. 2, *A Christian View of the Bible as Truth*. Westchester, Ill.: Crossway, 1982.

———. *A Christian Manifesto*. Wheaton, Ill.: Good News, 1982. Also in *The Complete Works of Francis A. Schaeffer: A Christian Worldview*. Vol. 5, *A Christian View of the West*. Westchester, Ill.: Crossway, 1982.

———. *The Church at the End of the Twentieth Century: Including, the Church Before the Watching World*. Wheaton, Ill.: Crossway, 1994.

———. *Death in the City*. In *The Complete Works of Francis A. Schaeffer: A Christian Worldview*. Vol. 4, *A Christian View of the Church*. Westchester, Ill.: Crossway, 1982.

———. *Genesis in Space and Time*. Downers Grove, Ill.: InterVarsity Press, 1972.

———. *The Great Evangelical Disaster*. Wheaton, Ill.: Good News, 1984.

———. *He Is There and He Is Not Silent*. Wheaton, Ill.: Tyndale House, 1972. Also in *The Complete Works of Francis A. Schaeffer: A Christian Worldview*. Vol. 1, *A Christian View of Philosophy and Culture*. Westchester, Ill.: Crossway, 1982.

———. *How Should We Then Live?* Westchester, Ill.: Crossway, 1983. Also in *The Complete Works of Francis A. Schaeffer: A Christian Worldview*. Vol. 5, *A Christian View of the West*. Westchester, Ill.: Crossway, 1982.

———. *Joshua and the Flow of Biblical History*. In *The Complete Works of Francis A. Schaeffer: A Christian Worldview*. Vol. 2, *A Christian View of the Bible as Truth*. Westchester, Ill.: Crossway, 1982.

———. *The Mark of the Christian*. In *The Complete Works of Francis A.*

Schaeffer: A Christian Worldview. Vol. 4, *A Christian View of the Church.* Westchester, Ill.: Crossway, 1982.

———. *The New Super-Spirituality.* In *The Complete Works of Francis A. Schaeffer: A Christian Worldview.* Vol. 3, *A Christian View of Spirituality.* Westchester, Ill.: Crossway, 1982.

———. *No Final Conflict.* In *The Complete Works of Francis A. Schaeffer: A Christian Worldview.* Vol. 2, *A Christian View of the Bible as Truth.* Westchester, Ill.: Crossway, 1982.

———. *No Little People.* In *The Complete Works of Francis A. Schaeffer: A Christian Worldview.* Vol. 3, *A Christian View of Spirituality.* Westchester, Ill.: Crossway, 1982.

———. *True Spirituality.* Wheaton, Ill.: Tyndale House, 1979. Also in *The Complete Works of Francis A. Schaeffer: A Christian Worldview.* Vol. 3, *A Christian View of Spirituality.* Westchester, Ill.: Crossway, 1982.

Schaeffer, Francis A., and C. Everett Koop. *Whatever Happened to the Human Race?* Westchester, Ill.: Crossway, 1983. Also in *The Complete Works of Francis A. Schaeffer: A Christian Worldview.* Vol. 5, *A Christian View of the West.* Westchester, Ill.: Crossway, 1982.

Schaeffer, Francis A., and Udo Middelmann. *Pollution and the Death of Man.* Wheaton, Ill.: Crossway, 1992. Also in *The Complete Works of Francis A. Schaeffer: A Christian Worldview.* Vol. 5, *A Christian View of the West.* Westchester, Ill.: Crossway, 1982.

Sire, James W. *The Universe Next Door: A Basic Worldview Catalog.* 3rd ed. Downers Grove, Ill.: InterVarsity Press, 1997.

Smart, Ninian. *Worldviews: Crosscultural Explorations of Human Beliefs.* 2nd ed. Englewood Cliffs, N.J.: Prentice Hall, 1995.

Sorokin, Pitirim A. *The Crisis of Our Age.* 2nd rev. ed. London: Oneworld, 1992.

Sproul, R. C. *Lifeviews.* Grand Rapids: Baker, 1990.

Vander Goot, Henry. *Life Is Religion: Essays in Honor of H. Evan Runner.* St. Catherines, Ontario: Paideia, 1981.

Veith, Gene Edward. *Postmodern Times: A Christian Guide to Contemporary Thought and Culture.* Wheaton, Ill.: Crossway, 1994.

Walsh, Brian J., and J. Richard Middleton. *The Transforming Vision: Shaping a Christian World View.* Downers Grove, Ill.: InterVarsity Press, 1984.

Wells, David F. *No Place for Truth, or, Whatever Happened to Evangelical Theology?* Grand Rapids: Eerdmans, 1993.

Wolters, Albert M. *Creation Regained: Biblical Basics for a Reformational Worldview.* Grand Rapids: Eerdmans, 1985.

APOLOGETICS

Chapman, Colin. *The Case for Christianity.* Grand Rapids: Eerdmans, 1984.

Craig, William Lane. *Reasonable Faith: Christian Truth and Apologetics.* Wheaton, Ill.: Crossway, 1994.

Evans, C. Stephen. *Why Believe? Reason and Mystery as Pointers to God.* Rev. ed. Grand Rapids: Eerdmans, 1996.

Geisler, Norman. *Christian Apologetics.* Grand Rapids: Baker, 1976.

Kreeft, Peter, and Ronald K. Tacelli. *Handbook of Christian Apologetics.* Downers Grove, Ill.: InterVarsity Press, 1994.

Lewis, C. S. *God in the Dock: Essays on Theology and Ethics.* Grand Rapids: Eerdmans, 1970.

———. *Mere Christianity.* New York: Touchstone, 1996.

———. *Miracles: A Preliminary Study.* Hammersmith, London: Fount, 1974.

McCallum, Dennis, ed. *The Death of Truth: What's Wrong with Multiculturalism, the Rejection of Reason, and the New Postmodern Diversity.* Minneapolis: Bethany, 1996.

McDowell, Josh. *Evidence That Demands a Verdict: Historical Evidences for the Christian Faith.* Vols. 1 and 2. San Bernardino, Calif.: Here's Life Publishers, 1990.

Moreland, J. P. *Scaling the Secular City.* Grand Rapids: Baker, 1987.

Novak, Michael. *Will It Liberate?: Questions about Liberation Theology.* Mahwah, N.J.: Paulist Press, 1986.

Phillips, Timothy R., and Dennis I. Okhom, eds. *Christian Apologetics in a Postmodern World.* Downers Grove, Ill.: InterVarsity Press, 1995.

Pinnock, Clark. *Set Forth Your Case: Studies in Christian Apologetics.* Chicago: Moody Press, 1971.

Schaeffer, Francis. *Escape from Reason.* Downers Grove, Ill.: InterVarsity Press, 1968. Also in *The Complete Works of Francis A. Schaeffer: A*

Christian Worldview. Vol. 1, *A Christian View of Philosophy and Culture.* Westchester, Ill.: Crossway, 1982.

―――. *The God Who Is There.* Downers Grove, Ill.: InterVarsity Press, 1968. Also in *The Complete Works of Francis A. Schaeffer: A Christian Worldview.* Vol. 1, *A Christian View of Philosophy and Culture.* Westchester, Ill.: Crossway, 1982.

Sproul, R. C. *Objections Answered.* Glendale, Calif.: Regal Books, 1978.

Sproul, R. C., John H. Gerstner, and Arthur Lindsley. *Classical Apologetics: A Rational Defense of the Christian Faith and a Critique of Presuppositional Apologetics.* Grand Rapids: Zondervan, 1984.

ETHICS

Bellah, Robert. *Habits of the Heart: Individualism and Commitment in American Life.* Berkeley, Calif.: University of California Press, 1985.

Eberly, Don, ed. *The Content of America's Character: Recovering Civic Virtue.* New York: Madison Books, 1995.

Finnis, John. *Fundamentals of Ethics.* New York: Oxford University Press, 1983.

Grisez, Germain G. *Beyond the New Morality: The Responsibilities of Freedom.* Notre Dame, Ind.: University of Notre Dame Press, 1988.

Himmelfarb, Gertrude. *The De-Moralization of Society: From Victorian Virtues to Modern Values.* New York: Alfred A. Knopf, 1995.

Kreeft, Peter. *Back to Virtue.* San Francisco: Ignatius, 1992.

Lewis, C. S. *The Abolition of Man.* New York: Simon & Schuster, 1996.

MacIntyre, Alasdair. *After Virtue: A Study in Moral Theology.* 2nd ed. Notre Dame, Ind.: University of Notre Dame Press, 1997.

Neuhaus, Richard John. *America Against Itself: Moral Vision and the Public Order.* Notre Dame, Ind.: University of Notre Dame Press, 1992.

Plantinga, Cornelius, Jr. *Not the Way It's Supposed to Be: A Breviary of Sin.* Grand Rapids: Eerdmans, 1995.

Plantinga, Theodore. *Learning to Live with Evil.* Grand Rapids: Eerdmans, 1982.

Sproul, R. C. *Christian Ethics.* Orlando: Ligonier Ministries, 1996.

Thielicke, Helmut. *Theological Ethics.* Vol. 1, *Foundations.* Grand Rapids: Eerdmans, 1966.

LIFE

Burtchaell, James. *Rachel Weeping and Other Essays on Abortion.* Toronto: Life Cycle Books, 1990.

Crutcher, Mark. *Lime 5: Exploited by Choice.* Denton, Tex.: Life Dynamics, 1996.

Grisez, Germain G. *Abortion: The Myths, the Realities, and the Arguments.* New York: Corpus Books, 1970.

Jacoby, Kerry. *Souls, Bodies, Spirits: The Drive to Abolish Abortion Since 1973.* Westport, Conn.: Praeger, 1998.

Larson, Edward, and Darrel Amundson. *A Different Death: Euthanasia and the Christian Tradition.* Downers Grove, Ill.: InterVarsity Press, 1998.

Lee, Patrick. *Abortion and Unborn Human Life.* Washington, D.C.: Catholic University Press, 1996.

Marshall, Robert, and Charles Donovan. *Blessed Are the Barren: The Social Policy of Planned Parenthood.* San Francisco: Ignatius, 1991.

Massè, Sydna, and Joan Phillips. *Her Choice to Heal: Finding Spiritual and Emotional Peace after Abortion.* Colorado Springs: Chariot Victor, 1998.

Olasky, Marvin. *Abortion Rites: A Social History of Abortion in America.* Wheaton, Ill.: Crossway, 1992.

ABOUT THE AUTHORS

Charles W. Colson graduated with honors from Brown University and received his Juris Doctor from George Washington University. From 1969 to 1973 he served as special counsel to President Richard Nixon. In 1974 he pleaded guilty to charges related to Watergate and served seven months in a federal prison.

Before going to prison, Charles Colson was converted to Christ, as told in *Born Again*. He has also published *Life Sentence, Crime and the Responsible Community, Convicted* (with Dan Van Ness), *How Now Shall We Live?* (with Nancy Pearcey), *The Body* (with Ellen Vaughn), *A Dance with Deception* (with Nancy Pearcey), *A Dangerous Grace* (with Nancy Pearcey), *Gideon's Torch* (with Ellen Vaughn), *Burden of Truth* (with Anne Morse), *The God of Stones and Spiders, Why America Doesn't Work* (with Jack Eckerd), *Answers to Your Kids' Questions* (with Harold Fickett), *Who Speaks for God?, Kingdoms in Conflict, Against the Night,* and *Loving God,* the book many people consider to be a contemporary classic.

Colson founded Prison Fellowship Ministries (PF), an interdenominational outreach, now active in eighty-eight countries. The world's largest prison ministry, PF manages over 50,000 active volunteers in the U.S. and tens of thousands more abroad. The ministry provides Bible studies in more than 1,000 prisons, conducts over 2,000 in-prison seminars per year, does major evangelistic outreaches, and reaches more than 500,000 kids at Christmas with gifts and the love of Christ. The ministry also has two subsidiaries: Justice Fellowship, which works for biblically based criminal justice policies, and Neighbors Who Care, a network of volunteers providing assistance to victims of crime. Also a part of the ministry is the Wilberforce Forum, which provides worldview materials for the Christian community, including Colson's daily radio broadcast, *BreakPoint,* now heard on a thousand outlets.

Colson has received fifteen honorary doctorates and in 1993 was awarded the Templeton Prize, the world's largest cash gift (over $1 million), which is given each year to the one person in the world who has done the most to advance the cause of religion. Colson donated this prize, as he does all speaking fees and royalties, to further the work of PF.

■   ■   ■

Nancy R. Pearcey studied under Francis Schaeffer at L'Abri Fellowship in Switzerland in 1971 and 1972 and then earned a master's degree from Covenant Theological Seminary and did graduate work at the Institute for Christian Studies in Toronto. She is coauthor with Charles Thaxton of the book *The Soul of Science: Christian Faith and Natural Philosophy* and has contributed chapters to several other books, including *Mere Creation, Of Pandas and People,* and *Pro-Life Feminism.* Her articles have appeared in journals and magazines such as *First Things, Books and Culture, The World & I, The Family in America,* and *The Human Life Review.*

Pearcey is currently a fellow with the Discovery Institute's Center for the Renewal for Science and Culture, in Seattle, and managing editor of the journal *Origins and Design.* She is policy director of the Wilberforce Forum and executive editor of Colson's *BreakPoint,* a daily radio commentary program that analyzes current issues from a Christian worldview perspective. She is also coauthor with Colson of a monthly column in *Christianity Today.*

HOW NOW SHALL WE LIVE?

helps Christians make sense of the competing worldviews that clamor for attention and allegiance in a pluralistic society. Pulling no punches, Colson and Pearcey show that all other worldviews fail to meet the test of rational consistency or practical application in the real world. Only the Christian worldview provides a rationally sustainable way to understand the universe. Only the Christian worldview fits the real world and can be lived out consistently in every area of life.

Weaving together engaging stories with penetrating analysis of ideas, *How Now Shall We Live?* helps Christians defend their faith and live out its full implications in every arena—the home, workplace, classroom, courtroom, and public policy. It is a defining book for Christians in this new millennium.

Resources available from Tyndale House Publishers that support the message and ministry of How Now Shall We Live?

How Now Shall We Live?: cloth

How Now Shall We Live? Study Guide: paper
Two thirteen-week Bible lessons to help Bible study groups absorb and apply the concepts of Colson's magnum opus

How Now Shall We Live? Audio Book: The abridged version on four audiocassettes

Answers to Your Kids' Questions: A guide to help parents know how to talk to their kids about the worldview issues they face every day

Complete adult and youth video curriculum is available from LifeWay Church Resources.

Order by writing to LifeWay Church Resources Customer Service, MSN 113, 127 Ninth Avenue North, Nashville, TN 37211-0113; by calling toll free (800) 458-2772; by faxing (615) 251-5933; or by e-mailing customerservice@lifeway.com.

Look for other books and materials based on *How Now Shall We Live?* from Tyndale House Publishers.

Visit these Web sites for more information:

Charles Colson's books and tapes: chuckcolson.com

Breakpoint: breakpoint.org

Prison Fellowship Ministries: pfm.org

Other books by Tyndale House Publishers: tyndale.com

Addresses for more information:

Terry White
Communications Department
Prison Fellowship Ministries
P.O. Box 17500
Washington, DC 20041-0500

Public Relations
Tyndale House Publishers, Inc.
351 Executive Drive
Carol Stream, IL 60188
phone: (630) 668-8300
fax: (630) 668-3245

The content of this series is drawn from the major sections of *How Now Shall We Live?* Shorter in length, more acessible to readers, and with added questions, these books are ideal for group study. Each book will help readers engage Colson's ideas and learn how to apply them to the world around them.

 *Developing a Christian Worldview of Science and Evolution:* paper

 *Developing a Christian Worldview of the Problem of Evil:* paper

 *Developing a Christian Worldview of the Christian in Today's Culture:* paper